The Summons

To Become

. . .

Rachel Chambers

Contents

Then those who feared the Lord talked often one to another;

And the Lord listened and heard it,

And a book of remembrance was written before Him

Of those who reverenced and worshipfully feared the Lord,

And who thought on His name.[1]

*   *   *

Chapter 1

OUR OPEN DOOR

"To be entirely honest, I know of nothing quite so boring as Christianity without Christ,"[1] says Major Ian Thomas. I couldn't agree more. Yet, I know nothing more exciting than living Christianity WITH Christ, and the result is what this story is about. We were ordinary people, living "normal" lives—not outstanding, famous, or flashy. And Christ was there. He, being God, chose to live with us by His own plan and determination, and to summon us to a life so "un-boring" that it has to be recorded. This great privilege stretched our ordinary lives beyond their natural boundaries, beyond our limited imaginations. Come on in, and I'll share some of it with you. As I begin I'd like to introduce you to the family.

Our home is the house with the open door. Those who know us best know that our family loves people—particularly the drop-in, kick-off-your-shoes type. The house is orderly, but not immaculate; the spirit, warm and fun-loving; the vitality and energy of it originate with Christ. We have been "The Chambers Home" since June 18, 1976. That was the day Jim and I, best friends, vowed before witnesses to live and love as One and to follow our God until death separated us. Our wedding verse declared it: "For this God is our God for ever and ever: he will be our guide even unto death."[2]

God established our home. I have no doubt. He also chose to bring others into it. I think ours was His expandable model, somewhat like an accordion. He enlarged it with children (Nathan, Anne, Megan,

1

Micah, Mary, and Rebecca—better known as "Becca"). Many others came and left, having shared our home for various times and purposes: five years of foster children, African orphans, sojourners, Harrison, suffering and broken people, friends, missionaries, and guests. We've left our door ajar so that you can also enter, look around and see the grace by which we live. You will find we are real, and you are welcome.

The kitchen calendar read February 1990. Jim was the head of our family-run business, Master Repair Services. He thrived when serving others with his hands: repairing, remodeling, and building. The business gave him a chance to provide for family needs and still satisfied his love for helping others. When workloads overwhelmed him, or when he needed a hand, I was there: bringing lunch, picking up supplies, painting, digging, roofing you-name-it—I did it.

Being together was then, and still is, a way of life for Jim and me. From the time we were dating, we were a team. We both loved children of any age, and wasted no time after marriage in expanding the apartment on Xenia Avenue into a home for OUR team, OUR family. We added three children while in that home: Nathan, Anne, and Megan.

Our ministry was a together-thing, too. We connected with our kids as AWANA leaders at church and as junior high youth leaders. Jim's love for sports gave opportunity to be the kids' soccer coach and referee. I became team statistician, sideline cheerleader, and uniform washer. In the spring, he helped the kids train for track; in the summer, Little League. His competitive spirit, nurtured in his own growing-up family of twelve children, could be heard at meets or games or family nights. Loudly. Embarrassingly so. I was from a quiet, reserved upbringing; he from more unreserved. Yet, I think his intense love of sports and competition is what shaped our family into a team—whether of two or of eight. He added the fun to family life. I added the structure.

I loved Jim: he was generous and unselfish, inclusive of others and warm spirited. He did not see himself as higher than others nor of having arrived. Rather, he was a growing Christian, a teachable student, a human being who made mistakes and forgave mistakes. In family life, he was a willing participant in diaper duties, homeschooling, and upon rare occasions, dish duty. He stimulated meal planning by asking, "What's for supper, hon?" and taught Bible, home skills, and industrial arts to our children. My favorite virtue was his great ability to respond to me, whatever my need, after a worn-out day.

As for me, my interests were: Jim and the children, homemaking, violin, personal Bible study, church league volleyball, and being a Junior High youth leader. My life was fulfilled, and I never lacked for things to do. I was truly blessed, and I knew it.

As for the rest of the family, I find it fascinating to review what we were at the time of the summons, bud and seed. We did not quite look like what we would become — and yet we were all there, the spiritual DNA in place, ready for God's transplanting, pruning and growing. We could not imagine what God was about to do with us, nor could we foresee what it would take to make us become closer to the likeness of our Father. The growing pains and nurturing from Him are what these frank stories are about.

This is some of what we were when God took hold of us for missions. Just as the disciples were barefoot fishermen, unrefined and untrained in anything but fishing, so Christ picked up the raw material of the Chambers and put us into His workshop. He intended to make us into something we could not visualize, something useful to Himself, a picture made from His own blueprint and creative skill. We were about to become something we were not.

＊ ＊ ＊

"For we are his workmanship, created in Christ Jesus
unto good works, which God hath before ordained
that we should walk in them."[3]

Nathan

Interests: God, soccer, trumpet, singing, working with his hands, quality relationships, serving and encouraging others

Strengths: sports, team player, optimism, memorization (poetry, verses)

Anne

Interests: God, studying, violin, homemaking, church activities

Strengths: deep thinker, spiritual insights, soft heart

Megan

Interests: piano, friends, babies, home, collections

Strengths: cheerful helper

Micah

Interests: drawing, cars, friends, thumb-sucking, maintaining clutter

Strengths: talking to people, frank, warm-hearted

Mary

Interests: smiling, people, playing

Jim and Rachel

Interests: God, church, family, sports, music, serving

Chapter 2

In the Living Room

It is significant that our family's call to missions happened in the living room, our most-used gathering place. In the figurative sense, our "Living Room" had been the house we'd built with our own hands, the family life that filled its rooms, the church where we served, and the quiet and predictable college town of Cedarville, Ohio. We loved life in this Living Room, settled on the couch of contentedness. Life was good. Routines were comfortable. Marriage was fun. We were happy. Kids were our delight. Serving God was our passion. Why get up?

In one word: GOD.

Each July our church hosted an authorization service for missionaries; and each successive year, Jim and I felt God tugging on our lives, giving us feelings of unsettledness and a desire to get off the couch. That, in itself, was not a summons from God; it was more like clearing His throat, getting our attention. We sat up from our happy sprawl, poised to move out. Mentally, we began pacing back and forth rattling doorknobs here and there, to see if any would open to the world of missions. Finding nothing wide and inviting, we sat back down on the couch in The Living Room, but it was disappointing and now uncomfortable.

I have never been a good "sitter," so I could not relax. I'd wanted to be in missions since I was ten. It was then in my own family's living room that my father had read us *Mary Slessor: White Queen of the Cannibals*. As a little girl on Dad's couch, I daydreamed of becoming

5

Mary; of floating down a croc-infested river in Africa's "uttermost;" of telling the dark man about my Savior. It had been my heart's desire, but I'd never sensed an open door to go there. Instead, I'd married Jim, a faithful but common man, not an adventurer, nor a gifted speaker, but a good, practical worker. He'd been willing to be in mission work since high school, had loved and served God faithfully, but caught no special attention as a candidate for worldwide ambassadorship. We were very plain. God alone looked into our hearts and saw our great desire for Him and for His service. Others saw us as we were: plumber, homemaker, servants, parents of a growing family, and Jr. High youth leaders. We were no big deal.

With these simple facts of life, it seemed almost surreal that God would stir our hearts and hopes to be missionaries. After all, missionaries were special in some way that we did not view ourselves. They could speak fluently to crowds and lead masses to Christ. They were brave, even to the point of martyrdom and grave sacrifice. They were the hero-stuff, like Knights of the Kingdom, riding off into the war. We were just—us—untried and unspectacular. If only we had known that it is not *what we are* that Christ sees, but *what He would make us become*. If only we had known missionaries without their "image," before their platform presentations, observed their lives *before* His calling. If only we had known GOD better, the God who does the choosing. "For you see your calling, brethren, how that not many wise, not many mighty, not many noble are called. But God *has chosen* the foolish ... to put to shame the wise; and God *has chosen* the weak ... to put to shame the things which are mighty, and the base ... and the things that are despised God has chosen ... that no flesh should glory in his presence."[1]

Despite ourselves in our "as is" mentality, God was choosing and summoning the plumber, the homemaker, and five children. My latent hopes to be a missionary were now becoming wildly alive. I wanted Jim to keep trying global doors, to peer into every opportunity missions had to offer. Just sitting back down and waiting some more did not "sit" with me.

Jim, on the other hand, did not want to get off the couch until he heard God on the matter. Seeing my zeal, he let me know in no uncertain terms that we were not going to pry any doors off their hinges just to see if they'd open. He also let me know that we would not be making new doors in walls. Can you tell I had passion? Being a concrete and methodical man, he wanted strong evidence that God's call into missions could be verified and substantiated beyond ourselves. Certainly it had to go beyond the personal desire to serve, or a childhood dream, or even the restless feeling of being uprooted. Jim was always careful with our family, not liking drastic changes or threats to any of us. So this call from God needed to be there, giving him assurance that departure from home, kin, and country had not been some personal or self-induced whim. He wrestled with himself: did he have it and not recognize it? All we knew was that we were unsettled and questioning. This was NOT fun. "The Summons" could not be vague or mystical rhetoric for Jim.

The desire and interest for serving in missions intensified. As Jim sat in The Living Room, he earnestly examined two Scripture passages. "Let a man so account of us, as of the ministers of Christ, and stewards of the mysteries of God…it is required in stewards that a man be found faithful."[2] Faithfulness was a concrete requirement, not some mystical revelation. If we were to be sent, our church would recognize this quality in us. As for our desires, there was more to consider: "This is a true saying, If a man *desire* the office of a bishop, he *desireth* a good work."[3] The word "desire" was the hook that drew him in. Then, in the following sentences of Scripture, some very measurable and objective qualifications had to match the desire he felt. These appeared to be part of a summons from God. Jim began to evaluate these character traits in his personal life as well.

One other significant question about God's call loomed in Jim's mind: his role in the ministry. Everyone "knew" that missionaries are public speakers, but Jim avoided getting in front of crowds. He related well to the reluctant Moses, "O Lord, I am not eloquent or a man of words…for I am slow of speech."[4] (i.e.: I can't think of something to say, especially impromptu!) As fundamental as it sounds, he wanted assurance that the summons to missions would be in sync with something he *could* do.

Our pastor, Paul Jackson, reinforced Jim's thinking: he assured Jim that the church would only send out those men and women who were already serving capably in a capacity of ministry here. Was there actually a place in missions for those who love to help more than to lead? Jim was unsure. The question plagued him incessantly. One day, he announced in exasperation, "I've told God I don't know what to do with all this! If HE wants me in missions, someone has to come to me with a specific job he wants me to do. Then I'll say yes!"

I confess. I closed my eyes so they wouldn't roll. "Jim, that's *not* the way it's done. You contact mission boards or missionaries and tell them what your situation is. See if they have a need that matches what you can do." I spoke as if I *knew*. We'd been listening for years to all those authorization services for missionaries. Their "calls" didn't sound like Jim's. "I don't know of *one*, single missionary (I enunciated these carefully) who had to be contacted in person *with a specific job* before he caught on that he was "called." I was feeling impatient sitting on the couch and dealing with indecision.

"I don't care how others do it, Rach. I *don't* know if what I'm feeling is God's call or not. He does. I need that assurance from Him before I can go."

I sighed and knew I could not—and would not—move him. God would. I did not know at that time how kind and sensitive God is to us in our limited understanding. The proverbial lightning bolt from heaven would have been an undeniably clear sign, but we would probably all have been toast—burnt toast.

As God understood Gideon's need for affirmation, so God understood Jim's. He met and called us on the terms Jim had requested. Larry Fogle needed someone for a building project in Central African Republic. This confirmation—combined with the stirrings of our hearts, circumstances, and God's own written speech—beckoned us to our feet. God's holy arm rolled up His sleeves to lift an entire family, sitting on a couch, to a distant room at the other end of His household. "The Lord has made bare his holy arm in the eyes of all the nations; and all the ends of the earth shall see the salvation of our God."[5]

I was ecstatic; Jim was purposeful. Once convinced that GOD wanted us, we were again in the living room, at 4130 US Rt. 42E, ready to share that news with our kids.

* * *

"Faithful is he that calleth you, who also will do it."[6]

Chapter 3

Out of the Living Room

Jim sat in the blue recliner across from me. I was on the couch with Mary on my lap; four-year-old Micah sucked his thumb at my feet. He was quietly taking in the family gathering and his dad's serious tone. Nathan, straddling the piano bench, had both eyes riveted on his dad, sensing something of significance was up. Anne, though twelve, was highly sensitive and intuitive, aware that Dad had called the family together for more than a mere chat.

"Kids, God has been doing something very special in our lives. Mommy and I believe God has chosen us to do a job for Him in Africa. I think God wants our family to be missionaries." He stopped to study the impact of his words upon the children.

Silence.

He continued, "It will mean we will need to leave our house here in Cedarville, and our church and our friends. We will have to live in a place that is not like this home." Jim was very gentle in breaking this idea to the children. "For us to leave, we will all need to do it together. It is not just Mommy's and my decision. It's yours too. We are family; we do things together." Again he paused to evaluate the children's reactions. "You would also be missionaries. Do you think you could do that?"

The thought lay there in the air. Anne mulled over her dad's words as she creaked back and forth in the old rocker. She was our deep thinker, our analyzer. My eyes moved to nine-year old Megan, our little energizer bunny. I anticipated her jumping in with the same head-on enthusiasm as she did most everything in life. Instead, she sat there in a frozen silence behind her Strawberry Shortcake glasses. Something was not digesting. Sick feelings from her heart expressed themselves upon her face. I confess: I didn't get it! Micah sucked his thumb, and Mary played naively with the buttons on my shirt. It was quiet enough to hear the clock tick for several minutes.

"Do you kids have anything you'd like to share?" Jim asked. "Do you think you might be willing to go?" The kids were so deep in thought; we couldn't necessarily anticipate a response. Maybe the question was too deep for starters. I tried to prime them, but my effort sounded more like an echo than an improvement.

"So what do you think about going to Africa?"

Nathan was the first to say something. He had always been an enthusiastic participant in anything our family did. "I think it's great! Like, what would we have to *do*?" Jim and I tried to imagine what we'd never seen ourselves. We *didn't really know* the day-to-day stuff without actually living there.

"I guess you just keep *doing* what you are *doing* now. You help Mom and me—like you usually do at home or at church; and you make friends with the African kids. They have soccer over there, you know. You could do *that*, and use *that* to tell your friends and teammates what you know about Jesus." That seemed reasonable and manageable. Nathan was like Jim: he wanted to know he could do it before he agreed to it. He looked satisfied. One down.

Anne remained quiet and thoughtful. Most of her decisions were evaluated by her priority in spiritual matters. She appeared to share Nathan's reserve about the ability to fill the role of missionary herself, but her positive response seemed motivated by a genuine love for God and a desire to please Him. She was willing to try. Two.

Meg still sat on the floor in quiet sorrow. An internal war of major proportions was going on, but I did not know why. "What about my friends?" I remember her voice was thin and her little chin quivered with emotion. At last my heart understood: Megan's friendships were at her core. The thought of leaving Heather and Becca—friends for as long as their lives had been—was too much. She knew no friends on the other side, much less their culture or language. She remained silent, struggling. I could not tally "three" yet.

Micah removed his thumb long enough to get out an essential question: would we get to see wild animals? Yes! And of course we had to list all the possibilities that might intrigue his interest, as well as the dangerous snakes. Safaris and airplane rides sounded like a great life to a four-year old. He said yes, he was willing to go. With talk of animals and family outings, the children's interest peaked. Mary, of course, was a shoo-in. She went willingly anywhere.

Jim directed the family focus. "But being a missionary doesn't mean we just go over there on a big plane to have a good time and see the animals. It means some big changes are going to happen to us. We can't just go over to Africa and be like we are here and now; "**over there**" is not the same as "**over here**." *WE* will have to change." Jim opened his Bible to 1 Corinthians 9:22, to the experience and testimony of our favorite missionary the Apostle Paul: "I have become all things to all men that I might by all means save some."

In kid-terms, Jim explained that "becoming" means "changing." One example was Jesus: He became "flesh" like us—God with skin on. He left his own, beautiful home to move into the new neighborhood of earth. In the same way, Paul became all sorts of things for all sorts of men, so that by all these changes, some could come to Jesus. When we became something different, we might not feel "normal," but it was God's way for us to reach people. Becoming all things meant we would become part of the African neighborhood. We would learn to eat food that might not look so appetizing to us. We might have to wear clothes that weren't our style. The kids would learn new games—African games, and communicate with a language we did not now understand. In short, becoming a missionary meant becoming willing to be something we hadn't been before—African. To the Africans we would become Africans, so that we might win them over to Christ and teach them how Jesus would live in Africa.

Nathan, Anne, and Megan were all old enough to absorb the abstract. Micah remained a concrete four-year old. He sat there taking it all in intelligently, sucking out all his mental juices from that thumb.

Jim continued, "So are we willing to make big changes? Do you think you could be willing to do that, for Jesus' sake?"

The kids were silent, thinking. There were thoughtful nods as each one came to his own decision. Meg had tears behind her glasses, still stiff in her struggle and incomplete in her thoughts. Micah had been contemplating all this talk of change. He had one, last, ominous concern. He removed the thumb-plug to release his ponderings:

"Daddy? Are we going to come back all black?"

The soberness of the moment was broken instantly—comic relief even for Megan. Micah was a bottom line guy. For a blonde, fair skinned four-year-old, he wanted to know: what are the limits to this "change?" The spirit of the room lightened while subconsciously we all wondered how much we *would* change. How much **could** we change? There was a sense of vulnerability and of our own limitations—more than we wished. All we knew was with God, *nothing* is impossible, even being changed into something we were not.

. . .

"I will make you [become]…"[1]

Chapter 4

New Images

The idea of becoming a missionary family took time to sink in. The position seemed to have an identity of professionalism—or at least an unvoiced expectation—that one knew what one was doing. I was expected to write prayer letters about "souls." Jim was expected to pound a pulpit instead of nail heads; the children were expected to behave and never embarrass the parents. We all struggled a bit with what we were supposed to look like, and since we did not know, nor could we live up to our own imaginations, we simply showed what we were. We were transparent.

After interviews and applications, a process was set in motion for us to contact churches who might be willing to support us. Jim and I prepared introductory portfolios of our family and ministry backgrounds for churches and supporters. Of course we needed a professional photo for the portfolio and prayer cards. This required the painful process of trying to capture this missionary image—whatever that was—in a studio setting. Fortunately, the photographers were a stick-together family like our own and friendly to the humors of polishing children's "moving parts." Kim Moser, both friend and curling iron queen, poked at and altered our "raw image" so that we looked somewhat real-to-life and acceptable. In retrospect, our clothes were formal, and we were over-dressed for authenticity, but then again, we were experimenting with impressions, not reality.

THE CHAMBERS
Serve the Lord with Gladness

Missionaries to the
CENTRAL AFRICAN REPUBLIC

Back at 4130 US. Rt. 42E, we did not think about image as much as our preparations as African missionaries. This was a mental adjustment as much as spiritual. Nathan and I were walking down McMillan Road one day, and I asked him, "What are you thinking about this new phase in our lives?"

"I really want to do it, and it's such an honor! But what I can't figure out is why GOD would want **US!**" He kind of spit out the "us." I don't think he was suffering from low self- esteem as much as from high expectations and lack of familiarity with this new concept. Did he forget there were other "commoners" whom God had called: David, a boy from the pasture; or Elisha, a farmer from the backside of his oxen?

I laughed quietly at his frank astonishment. "Yeah, I know what you mean. We sure aren't going to Africa because we deserve it, are we! But did you ever think that maybe God wants to show what He can do with just ordinary people?" He thought on that and seemed to relax some. The treasure of God comes in clay pots, containers that cannot praise their own magnificence. They can only delight in what is within, the Treasure Himself, and the One who shapes the pot.

We all struggled some with the idea of who we were, and who we were to become. We saw lumps—lumps of clay. He saw something more. The shaping began. Our first change was to become a family of sojourners. The mission process required that we travel from church to church, presenting the work we planned to do and the calling of our family into the ministry. The purpose was to create a support base financially and spiritually. As Jim had warned the children in the living room, change would come. Home routines had to shift to road habits, car living, mobile lifestyles, public rapport.

Nathan's sense of wonder at God's choice to use us set the tone and transparency for our platform selections. The children quoted Millie Crouch's poem, *"Me? A Missionary?"* (an incredulous and humorous reflection on becoming a missionary). We interspersed testimonies, Scripture, and songs, but it seems we were most remembered for our children's animated version of "Please Don't Send Me to Africa!" The chorus captured most people's feelings of African stereotypes and being called into missions:

Please Don't Send Me to Africa

Please don't send me to Africa!
I don't think I've got what it takes.
I'm just a man; I'm not a Tarzan,
Don't like lions, gorillas, or snakes.
I'll serve you here in suburbia,
In my comfortable, middle class life,
But please don't send me out into the bush,
Where the natives are restless at night![1]

Our children lip-synced the words and mimed the fears and expressions described in the song. Lions and snakes and Tarzan himself stood in contrast to our large family of vulnerable children. Perhaps that is one thing that accentuated the need for transparency and for God in our presentation. We sang, "Lord, I Need You," and people believed it. Our image as missionaries was not those of heroes, but of those in need.

Before the entire deputation process was finished, we had actually added another "bush babe" to the family—Rebecca. She was a surprise that accompanied a u-turn in the road. God changed our direction from the Central African Republic to Zambia. It was this experience—this change—that taught me the meaning of Proverbs 16:9.

* * *

"A man's heart devises his plans, but the Lord directs his steps."[2]

Chapter 5

Intentions and Plans

Jim's idea of someone calling him to complete a specific job affirmed that he was to contribute to missions in Africa. Larry Fogle's call for help initiated a direction for us, and we earnestly pursued raising support and preparing for Central Africa. It was a blizzard of activity for me: homeschooling children so we could travel to churches, preparing for a container to be shipped, and even taking some French and Sango lessons from Larry Fogle, now home on furlough. Our path seemed set, heads down to lunge across the finish line by August 1991. At least, that was the intention.

July 4th of the same year, shocking news came from the mission compound in the capital of Bangui. An unstable situation involving unpaid government workers caused rioting and pillage on the compound. The house where we intended to live was destroyed by fire. Other buildings were looted and ransacked. The Fogles and the other C.A.R. missionaries lost virtually everything. The mission shut down all possibility of short termers or first termers entering the country. We were devastated. It was like throwing all your weight in one, propelling lunge to cross the tape, but hitting a stone wall head first. We were stunned, hurt, and bewildered. After all the waiting, my childhood dream, the call, the affirmation, the year of road travel and topsy-turvy schedules—where was God in all this? I just could not process it.

Coming to our senses was a process. We felt like we were in the dark, groping on our hands and knees: "There's a path around here somewhere: we were JUST on it!" Secretly, I wondered if that path led back to the couch in The Living Room. I was depressed. How could we get this far just to be dumped by the mission at this point? I dreaded more waiting.

I went for a long walk with God, alone. My heart was so heavy, I could barely put one foot in front of the other. Our plans were history— nothing more. I had no sooner passed the end of our driveway, but I heard a still, small voice within, "My thoughts are not your thoughts; [That was comforting to a moper.] neither are your ways my ways. [This abrupt change was proof of that!] For as the heavens are higher than the earth, so are my ways higher than your ways and my thoughts than your thoughts."[1] At this point, I actually looked up. The grey sky held no boundary. For once, its measureless height declared to me a bold reality: God and I were not thinking on the same level about this. He was so far over my head that it could not be calculated! I felt a release from some of the heaviness. The rest of the walk was more of a monologue with the Lord, "whatabout...whatabout..." I was searching for something to satisfy my need to know. God was a steady listener, but He wanted trust, so He waited to answer.

Ironically or, should I say providentially, the mission's candidate training school was just weeks after the uprising in C.A.R. We met with mission representatives to reconsider our options. We "just happened" to see a presentation by Steve Bell, a man small in stature but big with strategic vision. He was opening a new country for the mission: Zambia. Several things compelled me in his presentation: the country was friendly, not war torn; we could speak English there; the climate was conducive to Jim's health. We went back to talk things over with our pastor, Paul Jackson. We trusted him. At his suggestion, we made initial contacts with the Bells by phone, beginning to investigate the field and what role we might play on the team.

By September, we had flights to Washington State to meet the Bells. I had just discovered that the shock of July's news had thrown off more than my mental and emotional balance. We were now expecting not only a change of field, but a change in the family! I did not greet this revelation with my usual joy; I'd had NO INTENTION of taking a tiny infant into deepest, darkest Africa, especially with over one quarter of the population being HIV infected; so much for intentions and my neat, little humanoid plans! The plane ride west was my one and only time to use those special, white bags for air turbulence. The two, blue Dramamine that Sallie Fogle had given me only assisted my first-trimester lethargy. Poor Jim! I was literally a sick deadbeat on a quest.

After arriving in Quincy, Washington, we focused on our goal: getting to know the Bells and determining if our participation with the ministry would be helpful. Getting to know them was a bit intimidating. Their rich heritage and experience in missions was the exact image that we had imagined we would have to have, but did not. Both Steve and Ruth Ann had grown up in missionary families in the former Belgian Congo now the Democratic Republic of the Congo. Ruth Ann and her family had served lifetimes in the jungle villages. In January of 1964, Congolese terrorists attacked the mission compounds where they served. Her Aunt Irene (Ferrell) had been killed in the raid, but Ruth Ann and her family were rescued by a UN helicopter. After the country stabilized, Ruth Ann's parents returned, as did the Bells, and some of Ruth Ann's siblings. The Bells, themselves, invested fifteen years in the DRC, working and living in remote settings with their three children, even adopting one of the Zairian children (Egiza) as their own. All were hearty workers and seemed accustomed to African life challenges. They spoke of killing snakes and playing in the jungle fearlessly. It was all very impressive and drawing, though we had a difficult time relating to it.

Five days and five pounds later, (too much conversational snacking) we loaded ourselves onto the plane. We felt there was potential for a new direction and an expanding role on the team. Our discussions revealed that the emerging team for Zambia had no one specializing in youth ministry, family counseling, or construction for the develop-ment of the new properties. Our past fifteen years as Junior High youth leaders, our backgrounds in Christian Education and Bible, and Jim's hands-on construction experience made this role credible for our church family. Pastor Jackson and the church affirmed that the role was appropriate to our current patterns of service: helping, teaching, building, and encouraging others.

Jim's *intentions* at the time of our call into missions had been to assist missionaries through hands-on construction projects. In the change of fields, he continued to pursue the idea of using construction for this newly developing field. Steve assured him that church buildings and housing for the new team would be essential. Again, God was thinking over our heads and our intentions: "I will build *MY CHURCH*,"[2] the organic body of Christ. His focus was on eternal buildings, houses not made with hands, churches not built with bricks and mortar. He was the construction supervisor and we "…laborers together with God"[3] Jim would learn to build churches as Paul described: "I have laid the foundation and another builds thereon. But let every man take heed how he builds thereupon. For other foundation can no man lay than that is laid, which is Christ Jesus."[4]

Our intentions and plans were both subject to God's mind. The alterations from our good intentions to God's intentions were revealed to us gradually and purposefully. He took the desires of our hearts, and spoke His will into the circumstances. He then confirmed it through His written Word, knowing that we can trust that implicitly. Though we had confusions and doubts at different stages, He made sure that we eventually understood enough to intelligently respond to what He had planned for us. "My sheep hear my voice, and I know them, and they follow me."[5] As He led us, He assured us, "I, the LORD your God, will hold your right hand, saying to you, "Fear not, I will help you."[6]

"Thou God of my end,
Thou hast given me a fixed disposition
To go forth and spend my life for thee;
If it be thy will, let me proceed in it;
If not, then revoke my intentions.
All I want in life is such circumstances
As may best enable me to serve thee in the world."[7]

* * *

"All the way my Savior leads me.
What have I to ask beside?
Can I doubt his tender mercy,
Who through life has been my Guide?
Heavenly peace, divinest comfort,
Here by faith in Him to dwell,
For I know whate're befall me,
Jesus doeth all things well!"[8]

—Fanny Crosby
(blind songwriter who knew what it meant to be led)

Chapter 6

Awe We Awmost Theya?

Once we had been approved to pursue team ministry in Zambia, we now had to raise the remaining support funds for living there. Getting back into the Chambermobile was less than inviting, but there were preparations of character and contentment to be learned here.

"Maumee! Ah we awmost theya?" Mary, our very bored two-year-old, yelled from the back of the van. "Maumee" was idly counting and categorizing road kill on this fourth day of deputation travel. "Van-itis" was clearly at epidemic proportions: Anne was chewing the end of her pencil as she stared through the Algebra book; Megan's mouth was hanging open in sleep; and Nathan was counting accumulated Wendy's napkins as he and Jim listened to NBA playoffs.

Micah and Mary had amused one another with silly faces, silly words, saliva bubble contests, and a gamut of books and games. Now it was up to me to announce that we were close to our destination—which we were not. I wondered if the Apostle Paul had anything comparable on his missionary ventures. If so, what would he suggest? This thought launched "Maumee" into an introspective analysis of deputation—negatives first, of course.

Imagine no deputation! Just pack up and go! Churches could contribute monthly to a mission fund from which approved missionaries would be supported. With funds already in place, we would not have to expend so much "mission energy" gathering resources. The idea sounded solid; I decided to develop a soapbox to escape my captivity in the van.

Now here's a thought: wouldn't missionaries be better equipped for ministry if we were rested and refreshed? With six children, I wasn't sure that EVER occurred, deputation or no deputation. Maybe that wasn't pertinent. We passed a skunk, belly up, and I tallied two. Back to my soapbox: let's see, if there were no deputation, we wouldn't have to repeat our slide production. I sure would love a meal-sized message in place of our warmed-over presentations. Thirty-six meetings in thirty weeks had left us feeling like a badly scratched 45rpm-record, very **R E P E T I T I V E…R E P E T I T I V E…r e p e t i t i v e.**

While I was evaluating, maybe I ought to consider the issue of missionaries competing for time, support, and effective presentations. That really bothered me. I appreciated the quality of servants I'd met in missions so far. Most seemed well-screened, faithful, and worthy of being sent, whether their presentations measured up to the expectations of the churches or not. A bloated groundhog interrupted my musings. Eight. Bad day for groundhogs.

The break in concentration was good. Some questions needed years of research, and today I was too tired to begin mine. Lunch and a rest area solved my immediate needs.

Back in the van, I was feeling brighter and amused myself with humorous memories of our many deputation experiences. Lost in myself, I laughed aloud. Immediately, twelve eyes focused on me. I joined the family in Reality.

"Oh, I was just thinking about Nathan at that Cleveland church."

"You mean when he walked through that door in the dark, and stepped four feet down into the baptistery?"

"Yeah," echoed two of the children. "One giant step for mankind."

"That WAS funny!"

"Not as funny as Mom walking into that one church with a curler still in her bangs." I heard giggling as I sobered some in embarrassment. Good thing that church had a good sense of humor. I wondered if they had noticed the toothbrush hanging out of my dress pocket during our platform appearance.

"It probably gave us 'authenticity' as part of the human race." I consoled myself dryly.

Deputation had more than its share of amusing adventures. We recalled as a family the time the car wheel fell off just as we were leaving (loose lug nuts); and another time we lost the door from its hinge right in the parking lot. God must have enjoyed that car! He used it frequently to illustrate His grace. I felt privileged that we could laugh about it together. God had given us safety so that the family's presence and participation at every planned meeting was possible. Because of our togetherness, we experienced unique joy. I liked family joy.

We passed something unidentifiable (new category: tally one). Since tallying seemed to pass the time effectively, perhaps I should choose new subjects… something nobler might be refreshing. Let's see… benefits and blessings of deputation? I agreed with myself.

I already had (1) FAMILY TOGETHERNESS (2) HUMOROUS EXPERIENCES and (3) SEEING GOD'S GRACE to begin my list. The next positive surely ought to be (4) SWEET FELLOWSHIP. Under this category I put memories of believers we'd met while traveling: the churches that cheered us on when we were discouraged; the host families who had befriended us; the many, sensitive ones who had slipped us monetary gifts or hugged us as we left; the tiny church which circled 'round our family in prayer and farewell. These were Christ's own kin, and very dear to us. We'd never have known them without deputation.

I was beginning to enjoy myself in the van. Memories were flowing freely. I thought of ten-year old Beth, an unkempt and neglected welfare child who hung onto our family one Sunday after morning service. She never left our side until 10:30 that evening, asking to wear our clothes and have her hair fixed with a curling iron. She'd whispered to my daughter, "I wish I lived with your family;" and to me she said, "You must be just like Jesus!" I had cried over that, feeling so unworthy of such a compliment. The little kindnesses we had shown made Matthew 5:16 come to life for us. I wouldn't trade that for anything.

I decided that number (5) of my list of blessings should read "MINISTERING TO OTHERS."

I thought of the SPIRITUAL BENEFITS we reaped because of our high visibility in ministry. Because we'd been transparent in our presentations, people were alerted to our needs, and prayed accurately and sensitively for us. When they prayed, we prospered. It was wonderful! Under this category I had umpteen examples:

- I had an unusually good delivery of our sixth child, Rebecca.
- Megan's broken arm mended in record time, amazing the orthopedic surgeon.
- We'd been delivered from temptations and hazards.
- Numerous provisions appeared just at the needed time.

It was all because faithful Christians in various churches prayed. Deputation introduced me to effective prayer partners. Yes, we were all better off. I was convinced. I thought of other categories under SPIRITUAL BENEFITS: personal growth, spiritual disciplines, ministry experience for our children. The goodness of God overwhelmed me…

"Maumee!" Mary drew out my name in a tired little voice. "Ah we awmost theya?" Despite the blessing of God, car weariness remained a stubborn reality, especially for little bodies needing to wiggle, **and** for Maumees. I slipped Mary the last car treat from my purse and praised the Lord we were within announcing distance. Once we were home, we could look back with a sense of triumph; another trip behind us, a few more blessings to tally.

⊕ ⊕ ⊕

"In everything give thanks, for this is the will of God in Christ Jesus concerning you."[1]

Chapter 7

Closing Doors Behind Us

By April of 1992, our financial and spiritual support base was strong. We purchased tickets to leave for Lusaka, Zambia on July 14th. The mission team flying out with us was to be Larry, Sallie, Aimee, Janine, and Ryan Fogle; Sherry Segal, and Doreen Lacy. Steve and Ruth Ann's family had already gone ahead of us in January to look for housing and to further prepare for the establishment of the team's ministry.

The spring prayer letters of 1992 read:

...we are in good spirits. Each of us is energized as we clearly see the goal of leaving and realize that God Himself has made this privilege possible. For the most part, we feel light-hearted; for the other part, a bit nostalgic. We look back to the beginning of this process and marvel at what God has done for us. Then we look around at family, friends, and our dear church, sensing anew how much we appreciate their presence in our everyday lives. A few tears are surfacing as we anticipate separation and unfamiliarity, but balancing that is the pleasure of doing God's will. In that, we find a consoling satisfaction.

While our minds and hearts fill with thoughts and mixed emotions, our bodies are busy with preparations: the house is getting fresh paint and repairs; and we're sorting through piles, hand-me-downs, keepsakes and accumulations. Necessary business is being completed (flight arrangements, passports, immunizations, etc.); and packing and purchasing has begun... A couple times each week, we learn about Zambia, its culture, customs, British English terminology, etc. I spend Thursday evenings with veteran missionary, Alice Wimer, learning from her experience in working with African women. Sherry Segal visited us for five days so that we could become better acquainted. She already is like family and we feel so thankful that she's part of the team.

As the months progressed towards summer departure, the activity escalated. Somehow we took time for our little "Thumper's" debut. Rebecca Lynn was born in the downstairs bedroom May 3rd, adding more adjustments to our whitewater schedules. Jim was working part time, helping pack, preparing the house for renters, and running us to appointments for immunizations, new baby checkups, and the dentist. Ah, the dentist! My journal read:

"Here I am, in the dentist's chair again, the fourth time in one week. Africa couldn't be much worse than the USA for discomforts. Seven days ago I had two fillings done and two wisdom teeth pulled. Yesterday, two teeth reconstructed; and today, the last three fillings. I've had so much Novocaine, I wonder if I'll regain feeling someday."

Feelings came all right. June 14th our church hosted our commissioning service. Our families, by bloodlines and birth, as well as 450 spiritual kin came to encourage and participate in our launching ceremony.

Commissioning Service at Grace Baptist Church, Cedarville

We sang Chamber music, "We Are An Offering," and I joined my two sisters and mother singing our prayer, "Take My Life." Both our dads recollected our growing experiences with God, and our pastors spoke encouragement to our church and to us. Our testimonies were printed on the back of the program:

JIM — It has been the hand of God working in my life over the years that has led me into missions. The training and example of my parents and the influence of other individuals have had tremendous impact upon my thinking. A growing relationship with God cannot be ignored, nor can the impact of godly pastors and laymen …. My wife has been a continual inspiration to me as we considered missions and waded through many discussions together. There is not one individual person or event that I could point to as having steered me into missions. God Himself has orchestrated it all and brought me to this juncture in life. I praise Him for that.

RACHEL — The opportunity to serve Christ is always a privilege wherever that may be. I consider this move to Zambia a privilege: it is God's response to our prayer to be used strategically in these last days. I thank Him for challenging me to expand my vision, my faith, and my personal experience in Christianity. I am particularly appreciative of the promise of His presence, His constant love, and His sufficient grace as we face a number of unknowns.

In the past months I have often heard: "My! You must be brave, going to Africa … and with a large family, too!" I assure you, the family's going is a non-negotiable; and the bravery I possess would not fill a thimble. I have struggled with many anxieties, but two things consistently influence me more than my fears and concerns. One is a greater fear of being disobedient or apathetic in my Christianity; the other is the factor of God's grace and love.

His grace has always enabled me at the time it was needed, and no one has ever loved me more or better than Christ.

I wrote in retrospect, "Emotions are fragile, but we're finding God's grace to be real. The night was filled with togetherness, remembrances, challenges, sweet music and prayer. It was a send-off to be remembered with fondness and gratitude."

The last month in the States was a series of closures. At my last dental appointment, I looked forward to closing my mouth as well as our house. "As I sit here in this dental chair, eleven ladies are in my house painting and cleaning. I don't think I could explain why I am happy. I surely don't like dental pain, or messes in the house, or people *seeing* my messes, but I do like that finality of closing up affairs here to begin a different phase of our lives. Circumstances do NOT dictate my joy. We are in His presence today, and there is fullness of joy. (Psalm 16:8, 9, 11)"

I knew that closure with family, church, and friends had to come; and I postponed the pain of separation like I'd postponed my dental checkups. Eventually, it could not be imagined away or avoided. We were all facing the inevitable last times together: last meals, last hugs, farewell notes, a memory book from our Sunday school class, a bucket of chocolate chip cookies, gifts of love not soon forgotten. Megan's Heather, Becca, and Laurie stuck to her like friendly Velcro, spending every day or night together "for one last time." Micah's friends were less aware of the significant separations, but each child was feeling his security strings loosening. Though Jim and I were there for them, each child had to individually walk through his own feelings and losses. This was a testing of their own personal decision some eighteen months earlier, the decision to become a missionary family. This is when I appreciated more than ever Jim's foresight to involve the children in the choice to face God's call together.

We made a quick trip to New York for farewells to Jim's family.

Journal entry, July 9, 1992:

We just cried through our goodbyes to Jim's parents and siblings.

It was very hard on all of us… Dad told Jim and me separately that no matter what happened, he was the happiest of men because we were going and were faithful to the Lord's leading. It is consoling to know that our parents share our joy of ministry and our commitment and love for Christ. Thank GOD for them! Bless them, we pray! Andy told Jim, "You've been a real example to me." There were many tears and expressions of love. Dad said that he thanked God for me, and that I'd been a wonderful helpmeet to Jim. I said, "Oh, he probably could've gotten better." Dad replied, "God only makes a few, honey." These are precious words to me. So were his tears.

All the older children had a hard time saying goodbye to Grandma and Grandpa. They have the blessing of knowing they are well loved and sincerely prayed for. I was happy to see Anne take the initiative to hug and cry with both Dad and Mom. She has deep feelings, though more reserved in expressing them. Mary, Micah, and of course Rebecca were unaware of how long and far away the separation would be. They were smiling and yet quietly curious as they observed the tears and sensed the spirit of the room.

Daddy announced last pit stop opportunities. Mary provided some comic relief when coming from her turn in the bathroom. Gramma's spare toilet paper holder, a doll whose crocheted skirt concealed the spare TP roll, was hiding inside the lavatory cupboard. "Gwamma, see the little girl? She's waiting to go pawty." Everyone laughed. It felt good after all the emotional heaviness. Then she was off, bolting to the Chambermobile in order to beat Micah.

We returned to Cedarville for other precious farewells with friends and church. That last week, I sat in the living room next to Becca's Pack 'n Play. The house looked barren and hollow from emptiness, more like an institution than my own, familiar home. It felt unbecoming like that. The memories of this house turned over like pages in a scrapbook: our family construction crew, including my grandpa and my parents; the completion of it as we lived here; the foster children; the two homebirths in the downstairs bedroom; celebrations and cakes and people. Closure of this home was not like discarding old tennis shoes. I was looking at a closure of something held dear. Yet we'd given this house to God before we ever built it. Both Jim and I had vowed we would not let our lives be controlled by love of things or even love of home.

The phone rang. It was Les, Jim's brother, a pastor in New York State. He was calling to encourage us, he said. Then, being Jim's "big brother," he confessed that he had to get in the last word. He said he'd been reading his Bible and thinking about what we were going through. The emotion was in his voice as he read Jesus' words to us, "There is no man that has left *house* or brothers, or sisters, and mothers and children and lands for MY sake and the gospels, but he shall receive a hundred fold now in this time, houses, and brethren, and sisters, and mothers, and children, and lands, with persecutions; and in the world to come, eternal life."[1] That was the real point God wanted me to realize. I could not leave anything at all—the dearest of relationships, even this house—but what I would be compensated one hundred times. Now that the departure time had come, the promises of God, not yet realized, were to be grasped. I thanked Les quietly. God, Who Himself is touched by the feelings of our weaknesses, sent me that message by phone. I cannot, and will not, forget it.

It was now time to pack up or store the last possessions. Jim had built a storage room at the back of our garage for our furniture and belongings. Once the mattresses were stored in there, we moved into our neighbors'/friends' house, the parents of Heather. It was a sensitive move on God's part to allow Megan's last night to be spent with her best friend.

Monday morning, we met in the church parking lot to load our belongings into the church's fifteen passenger vans—sixteen trunks, eight carry-ons; the Pack 'n Play, Umbroller stroller, and other paraphernalia. STUFF was an unbelievable mass. I justified it with the thought that I was going to the ends of the earth where there was no OTHER STUFF. Part of me questioned how much of this was necessary, but the "what ifs" plagued me. What if they don't have cribs in Africa? Yes, the Pack 'n Play had to come. Preparing for the unknown and the unseen had triggered overkill and my imagination. It was amazing that I had not packed even more, yet my love for simplicity felt annoyed with it all.

The parking lot farewell was a precious scene for us. Grace Baptist friends and family all gathered together to watch our send-off, giving and praying and encouraging us in the surreal moments. Some were even traveling the six-hour trip to the Chicago airport! Our bonds were strong. Our church family was tight! We were so grateful, so comforted as we drove out of Cedarville, our Living Room.

My sister's home was about an hour from O'Hare airport. Family was gathered there—cousins, siblings, Mom and Dad Mayo.

Monday (July 13ᵗʰ) was the perfect closure for our family. Dad fixed steak on the grill at Lin's and splurged on me with all the bing cherries I could stand… Bec made a perfect blueberry-peach pie. After dinner we all shared very happy memories, our best. We laughed together. It seemed like we were all saving sorrow for tomorrow, when there was no choice about parting. I don't remember even talking about the inevitable departure. Everybody was aware of it, and nobody wanted to bring it up. I only suffered lumpy throat syndrome. After supper, we gathered in the family room. Dad read from Scripture passages of other send-offs and separations: Elijah and Elisha, Jeremiah, Paul and the Ephesians. Dad shared a tape of a missionary to Brazil, his life story and song, "Take Everything But My Lord." I haven't the life to sing that worthily yet. I must love Him better and more!

As I walked to the house where we were to sleep for the night, I felt "finished" with the USA, and ready for my new home, one more out of a hundred promised in that verse.

Chapter 8

No Turning Back

The trip to the airport the next day was somewhat silent. No one seemed to think of something significant to say. We made small talk in the airport lobby with family and the rest of the arriving Zambia team. Then small talk became all business. We had to weigh and check 103 pieces of luggage plus two dogs in cages. Moving fifteen Americans across the globe was no small issue. With all the distractions, it was handy that Sallie and I had agreed to color coordinate the children in red T-shirts. They were easy to spot.

Once we were checked in, the entire entourage of cousins, Grandma and Grandpa, aunts and uncles, and Paul and Marilyn (dear friends from Cedarville) surrounded us as we made a mass parade to our departure gate. Mom played with ten-week old Rebecca, making her smile with bounces and baby talk. We kept ignoring boarding calls until the word "final" was attached to the announcement. At this point, tears were threatening composures. It was time. Dad gathered everyone together, and we prayed, arms around one another. Clinging embraces, last notes, and whispered messages passed among us. My heart felt like it was about to rupture. I tried to fix everyone's face in my memory, the scene, the love, the tears.

Jim gave the signal that we HAD to get through the gate now. I was overloaded worse than a gypsy: my carry-on, the Umbroller stroller, my violin, the diaper bag, last-minute gifts. In response to Jim's lead, I headed for the security gate.

A Gathering of Cousins

Mom called out, "Rachel! Did you forget something?" She was always saying that to me. I looked at her blankly. She was holding out Rebecca. Oh my word! Where was I supposed to put my daughter! I was mortified by my stuffed arms and absent-minded parenting. Mom draped Rebecca over the arm with the gift bags and diaper bag, and I headed for the security check. I walked somewhat sideways, somewhat backwards so I could continue to wave and to see the faces of family one last time. Jim was already through security, calling with urgency, "Rachel! You have to hurry!"

Still, I could not face forward; it would mean turning my back on family. I just could not do it. It seemed symbolic.

"Rach! YOU HAVE to turn around! We HAVE to go! C'mon!"

Jim's urgency could not be ignored. I had to turn to face Jim and the children; my back was to my family. At that point, I felt my heart tear away, like flesh from bone, as John Bunyan says. Inwardly I reached for my Father, like a hurt child reaching with both hands for comfort and security. Immediately, a sense of God's presence surrounded me. I don't know any more descriptive word of it than the simple word "sweet." His presence had enabled me to do what *I, in myself,* could not do. Surrounded by this sweetness, I faced the ramp to the plane. I felt such satisfaction, a satisfaction of obedience and Christ's pleasure. One final wave, and we disappeared from family and friends, but Christ's presence remained, too close for discomfort.

Getting all fifteen team members settled into seats and storage bins made quite the scene. Our family alone was a spectacle. The French stewardesses eyed Rebecca, draped over my arm among the other cluttered hodgepodge of last minute gifts. She remarked in her soft, French voice, "You have too many of se carry-ons. Sey will not fit into se ovahead beens." Larry Fogle stepped in to explain that we were going to Africa for two years, and that these were all needed. The stewardess softened a bit as I looked at her with apologetic relief.

"Here, let me take zeh babay!" she said, as if rescuing Rebecca from me. She took my little treasure down the aisle to show her off to the other attendants, and I untangled myself from straps and bag handles. To myself I spoke with no-nonsense resolution: "I will NEVER again travel with all this clutter. I would rather go without, than live weighed down like this!" I felt like I was trying to run a spiritual race dressed like the local peddler, strapped with encumbering weights. A very precious moment with God had been disturbed by STUFF. It wasn't worth it.

That resolution was my "noble moment." Now my mind argued between sacrifice and logical needs: the baby's bed, my violin, my personal belongings, and children's things had already been pared down to minimums. I was just so annoyed by material things at that moment—perhaps misplaced vengeance on myself for overlooking Becca. The stewardesses accommodated us kindly, but the experience burned an impression on my soul. "Life does not consist in the abundance of the things he possesses."[1]

The children did not sleep well on the plane—too excited. They were totally shot after our eight hour flight. Larry and Jim had the insight to rent rooms at an efficiency hotel at the Paris airport. The snug quarters were appropriately named, "The Cocoon." Each suite was about eight-foot square, consisting of a double bed and a two-foot bathroom, which meant one was able to fit both feet into the room at the same time—if you wore less than size 10 shoe. We lay down to rest, like breadsticks on a baking sheet, five at a time. There wasn't space for me, so I sat in the corner and propped my head against the wall to doze. Lack of sleep, a fussy baby, and drained emotions left me slightly cranky. I held it in, because NOW I was a missionary, and I didn't think I should be feeling like that.

After a few hours of modified rest, we were supposed to emerge as beautiful butterflies. The girls brushed their hair, polished their faces with wet wipes, and smoothed out wrinkled travel wings before flitting out of the cocoon for fast food. My journal recorded that "It cost us over $25 for seven plain hamburgers, two fries, and seven waters. Waters cost us as much as the burgers! We just paid for expensive indigestion!"

Everyone was eager to see the sights of Paris. We bought tickets for the subway and a boat tour on the Seine River. The Eiffel Tower, The Bastille, the cathedrals, and all the cultural arts were stimulating enough for our attention. But, I simply could not keep myself awake once we sat down for the tour. I was too exhausted to enjoy it fully. At the end of the day, we dashed back to the airport to catch our 11 p.m. flight. A midnight supper on the plane was greeted with the same sleepy enthusiasm.

The flight to Zambia was thirteen hours of very fussy little girls. Once they were over tired, they could not relax in the unfamiliar surroundings. I spent hours trying to keep them from fidgeting and disturbing other night travelers. The rest of the time, I was fighting with my own fatigue and agitated brain: I wanted sleep, but only found deprivation. I did not feel positive emotions until the navigator announced that we would be landing in Angola to refuel before heading on to Lusaka.

As the plane descended to the runway, the children were pressed against one another, vying for a window view of Africa. My own first impressions gave me a weird feeling, like I was breaking into a story-book that had never before been reality. I felt more like I was watching a National Geographic special, rather than living real life. The landscape was scrubby and dry and red, with crude stick fences and small garden plots scattered around primitive housing. African kids played barefoot by the runway. When the plane stopped, Angolan airport workers descended on the plane to clean it. Their uniforms and shoes had holes, a sign of the standard of living there. The whole scene jolted me a bit. We were actually IN Africa. I felt trembling and full of adrenaline.

Two hours later, we were landing in Lusaka. My stomach was doing flips as I eyed the brown landscape, parched from drought. It was barren looking. We entered the airport reception area, gawking at everything. Steve Bell met us in the restricted area, having gained special permission to help us through customs and the paperwork. What a welcome sight!

It took two trips in his huge, army-green Mercedes Benz truck to transport people and goods to the Bells' home nearby. My first impressions were not what I had thought Zambia would look like. There were strange combinations of modern roads and poorly clad Africans warming themselves next to evening fires. I didn't see huts, but then, I did not expect that! I didn't really know what to expect.

After unloading luggage and acclimating the children and dogs to their new surroundings, we ate a refreshing lunch and piled back into the bed of the army truck. Steve had gone to great lengths to find one property that might accommodate the entire team. It was in a suburb at the outskirts of the city, forty-five minutes from the Bell's home. The title sounded a great deal grander than it actually was. My first letter home described my impressions:

Our property is three acres, three houses, a chicken coop, well, and big-time junk sitting all over. Our proposed house is quite spacious and dirty, very African in taste and lifestyle. The kitchen has gaudy blue walls with bright orange cupboards. The five bathrooms are gold, blue, hot pink, 1950's-green. The bedrooms are all in odd colors as well. The house has several broken windows, dirt, cockroaches and…potential… I think! I have to admit, the visual impression challenged my creativity! I turned to Sallie and said with dry wit,

"Well, what d'you think? I can hardly make up my mind whether to go Victorian or Country." So this was to be the first of my one hundred houses!

Returning to the Bell's home, we each moved into our temporary "homes." Steve and Ruth Ann had graciously divided their four-bedroom home among all twenty-one of us: we took the largest bedroom since we had the most occupants. All seven beds fit together like a field of mattresses. Suitcases were in the corners, leaving a mere footpath for exiting and entering the room. The Fogles had a smaller room; Steve and Ruth Ann one; and the last was for Sherry and Doreen. The Bell's children and the American dogs, in their cages, occupied the living room. Somehow we were all in and accounted for by supper time.

After a wonderful meal, the wives were asked to make a grocery/supply list for the next six months. Yeah, right! The guys were to leave for South Africa by six in the morning to get supplies, appliances, and vehicles. I looked at Jim with dead-pan disbelief. After thirty-one hours of travel, minimal sleep, culture shock, and a roaring headache, I was supposed to KNOW what to put on a six-month grocery list? I had no idea what we needed; what supplies were available, the cost, or quantities. I was mentally about as sharp as a marble by then, and Becca had "had it" for the day.

I left my empty list and blank brain in the kitchen to nurse Rebecca in our room. She was exhausted when I laid her in the Pack 'n Play. As I arranged the mosquito net across the top of her bed, a huge spider darted across the wall next to her. I froze. It looked threatening. What if it was poisonous? I had to kill it, but I was scared to death. I thought of calling Jim, but reasoned that I was more than one hundred times bigger than that spider. "Besides," I told myself, "I'm a missionary now. I'm supposed to take care of these things. I have to be brave!"

Never taking my eyes off the spider or Rebecca, I felt around for the edge of the bed. Underneath was my sandal. I firmly grasped the sole and wound back for my attack. I was paralyzed with fear! He was so fast! What if I missed? I sucked in air and held my breath, drawing back again to strike. Rebecca stirred, and I feared waking her. I feared more for her safety. There was no turning back. I hit the wall with such solid force that I was surprised the cement plaster stayed intact. Next, I ground the sole into the cement just to be sure no living cell had survived. Lifting the shoe, I checked the enemy: he was dead, and my baby was safe. I let out my breath in a sigh, feeling triumph over fear.

Walking back to the kitchen, I announced in triumph, "I just killed a huge spider!"

Everyone looked up from their conversations. Brian Bell asked what kind. I just shrugged, and tried to describe him. Brian rolled his eyes in disgust. "That's just a flattie. They're harmless, and they eat the mosquitoes. You aren't supposed to kill them." I could see he thought I was stupid. His mom gave him a warning look that said, "Drop it," and Brian left the room.

I felt stupid, particularly as I sat down to try and assemble a purchasing list for South Africa. My only benefit in spider killing was that I now had enough adrenaline to stay awake. Ruth Ann helped the rest of us determine basic food needs and quantities. Jim asked questions that would help him know my preferences for dishes, appliances, and foods.

As soon as I could bow out, I did. Jim followed, bringing the children from their game playing in the living room. It didn't take long for everyone to fall asleep, except me. I lay there listening to gunshots outside the wall fence. Jim woke up and commented that Steve had said we were to just stay still; there would be gunshots almost every night. I'm not sure that helped me relax, but I began to think about that sweet presence of God that I'd felt at the security checkpoint. He was still here with me. Two more spiders, flatties, darted out from the storage units above the closets. I decided to name them Jezebel and Gertrude to give them personalities and less threat. At some point in time, I fell asleep, listening to my family's deep breathing.

Chapter 9

Launchings

The next morning at dawn, the men gathered outside the house for prayer before leaving for South Africa. Jim was less than excited to be leaving the children and me for a three-week absence. It seemed too much adventure for his routine-loving, home-centered disposition. The nightly gunshots probably did not encourage thoughts of safety and well-being either. This, too, had to be committed to the Lord in prayer. After one last kiss and hug, he loaded into the army truck with Larry and Steve and waved goodbye as they drove out the gate. The women and I returned to the kitchen for tea.

It was going to be interesting, running one household with five women, thirteen children, five rival dogs and no men. Paul Banda, the house help, and Henry the night guard who was often reprimanded for sleeping on the job, were our only human protectors. Fortunately, I was the only new-be on the team; I could glean experience from the other veteran missionaries, who seemed to take separations in stride. They were constructive with the situation and shared ways we could help each other: dish-washing, meal help, chore and devotion schedules, and assigned days for using the one washing machine. Since the Bell's electricity was most often on brown-out levels, the machine was only good before dawn or after bedtime. I determined to make my African experience, including the washday, the adventure it was going to be.

Meanwhile, Jim and the men were encountering their own real tastes of Africa: border crossings and corruption with officials. Steve determined it would be best to leave the Zambia-Zimbabwe border and backtrack a bit. The Zambia-Botswana border followed more closely to protocol, with fewer fees. While it lengthened the trip, his experience proved to be best. Three men on an all-male shopping spree turned adventurously wild: they spotted wild elephant herds, wild boar, antelope, monkeys, and more. Sherry flew down to Johannesburg to join the men in purchasing vehicles and supplies. The plan was for all to caravan the vehicles on the return trip.

Back in Lusaka, our own wild life was just getting underway. While I appreciated the security of the Bell's home and the wall fence, there wasn't much to do once daily chores were done. I needed to venture out, to see beyond the four walls and yard. I was a missionary now, and I wanted to be with the Africans. With Rebecca in my arms, I asked Henry to open the gate. As I stepped through the opening, the Zambian children stopped playing to stare at us, actually, more at Rebecca. I stared back. And then I just smiled at them. Immediately, we were surrounded by curious eyes, bright smiles, and dark, dusty hands. They were reaching out, patting us, touching her soft skin. Rebecca and I clung to each other, a little overwhelmed. A couple teens joined the crowd, and then a passing mother, and another couple ladies. One girl reached under Rebecca's arm to take her from me. Little kids were putting their dusty fingers into her mouth! I felt out of control, a little afraid.

It didn't seem right to be a missionary and to hold a fear of the very people I was to love, or I should say, the very ones Christ loved so dearly. Outwardly, I held composure, but inwardly, the old, nagging fear of HIV resurfaced. I didn't know which ones had it or TB or other diseases, and which ones didn't. This felt like a risky game of Russian roulette, only the target was my ten-week old baby, my family, myself. My maternal instincts and fears were at war with my faith, even my logic!

As I looked at the bright eyes and sweet faces, a little voice in my head was counting "One, two, three, four. HIV. One, two, three, four. HIV." (The rate of infection for Zambia.) These were the people behind the statistic, so friendly and open and warm. Why was I afraid? I had to answer myself—later.

Rebecca and I remained outside the gate, greeting the children and answering polite questions from the women who spoke English. One of them, noticing the clamor and unruliness with Rebecca, gave a motherly rebuke to the crowding children. Some returned to their play, but most remained curious over the white baby, touching and patting her everywhere. As we turned back towards the gate, a greater fear attacked my mind: what if I turned out to be a flop? Fear was a grave enemy of love. How was I going to get over it? Certainly not by denial, that was for sure! I stepped back through the wall-fence gate into surreal security, thoughtful. I faced both an internal challenge and a great opportunity.

Our new life held daily encounters. My journaling letters tried to capture the experiences:

July 20, 1992:

Today was the Chamber's washday. I felt like I'd stepped into a time capsule as I spent the entire morning with the "Chambermaids," squatting on African stools over metal tubs of suds and duds. I got the biggest tub, the bathtub. My least favorite was doing diapers and socks in the bathtub. I am going to lose the battle for a white wash. Bleach, called Jik here, is not working; the iron/rust from the well stains Bec's new diapers a dingy orange-yellow. I will not make Better Homes and Gardens' Homemaker of the Year award!

Sunday we all walked to the AME church building at 7:45 a.m., a place the Bells rent for the new church start. Someone was sprinkling water on the dirt floor. It seemed odd to me, until I was told that it holds the dust down. Women and children began drifting into the room.

Ruth Ann began the service with the singing of hymns. Worship for me was pure and refreshingly sweet. I sat on a four-inch-wide bench singing "It is Well with My Soul" accompanied by Ruth Ann's accordion. I could not remember a time when my soul had been "weller." I was right where God had placed me, and He was so near. I felt pure contentment and joy! I cried several times during the song service ... just because.

Then we were asked to bring special music. Because we'd sung our way through deputation, we had a repertoire of songs prepared. I chose the simplest of our family songs, "I Love You, Lord." It seemed to express my heart and required no accompaniment. The children filed up to the front of the church with me and began, "I love you, Lord, and I lift my voice to worship you ..."

As our harmony lifted into the room, my eyes glanced over my children. Megan stood in the front, her arm in a sling, her glasses sliding down her pug nose. In the very midst of spiritual pleasure, a fear seized me—a realization. Megan, my little musician, my gifted pianist would never have a piano or a good teacher or develop to her musical potential in Africa. What kind of parent was I? Why hadn't I counted the cost for the children? The thought came so instantly— right there in the middle of that worship song. My voice kept singing, but my heart froze. My thought scratched my tender soul like a speck on an eyeball. I could hear my own voice urging me, "Oh my soul, rejoice! Take joy, my king, in what you hear...."

In this new fear, the Comforter came to me. He gave me the mental picture of the children of Israel in a scrub brush wilderness for forty years ... shoes never gave out, water poured from a rock, bread rained from the sky. It was a solid fact from a solid God. So simple, but it gave me instant assurance that He could provide something for my Megan, and make something of her after all, somehow, some way. I laid my Megan before the Lord, in a private love offering to Him— her talent, her needs, her love for music, my motherly desire to see her prosper. I trusted God and finished the song in complete harmony of soul, "May it be a sweet, sweet sound in your ears." We returned to our seats as the people broke into delighted applause. No one knew what real worship had broken through to God during that short time span—no one but God and me. I sat down, very much at peace.

In the absence of male leadership, Ruth Ann led the service in testimonies, prayers, songs, and Scripture readings, directing the focus towards God. I thought back to some of my ponderings about worshipping in Africa. I'd wondered if dirt, bugs, crude circumstances, or even the people would distract me from knowing or enjoying God Himself. It didn't. That verse from Hebrews proved itself in the morning's experience: "Be content with such things as you have. For He Himself has said, 'I will never leave you nor forsake you.'"[1] Christ's presence filled me with sweet contentment and speechless joy! My worship felt so pure.

The July 20th letter continues:

> *I gave my testimony in the teen class. The Bell's house helper had only been saved for three months, but he led the class anyway. Even as a spiritual infant, the Spirit of Truth and forthrightness was in him. He stopped his "teaching" to ask my explanation of the verses he was learning for the first time. Another new convert, Collins, was bright and eager, like a bawling newborn whose appetite was ravenous. I loved it, just as a spiritual mother delights in satisfying her children. I was asked to lead the class in the 4:00 service. Again, they hung on every word I shared. When we closed, Paul, the house helper, prayed so earnestly and genuinely and gratefully, "Thank you for sending the Chambers family to us." In this dusty place, I felt significant.*

In the afternoon I visited the home of a girl I'd met at church. Monica lived with eight others in a two-bedroom house. Ruth had informed me that Monica was the key to the neighborhood. Everyone knew her. Her mother and family received me cordially, showing off their tiny, cement-block home and postage-stamp yard. We had tea together, and I shared pictures of our commissioning service with her. I mentioned that I would like to start a class for girls, teach them some skills, and have a Bible study. She said she wanted to learn sewing and volleyball, so I said, "Fine. Maybe I could teach that." The emphasis was upon the word "maybe" in my mind. The next thing I discovered, she'd told everyone that I was starting a sewing class for girls. That hit a community artery. I had a flow of community girls calling me to the gate, wanting to know me, asking when we could start. One morning, a man showed up at the gate asking for Mrs. Chambers. He said he'd heard we were starting a tailoring class and, of course, he wanted to join. Right about then I decided not to let on that I really don't like to sew at all. Me? A seamstress? Do I really have to become **all things**? I felt myself wincing.

July 22, 1992:

The children have adjusted well and are getting along with the MKs and Africans. Nathan played soccer today at the local school. He said the boys didn't pass to him very much, and they don't speak English on the playing field. Egiza was good to help bridge the obvious gaps. We are all trying: we all play volleyball daily with the neighbor kids in the Bell's yard. Rebecca has not completely adapted to the black faces: she cries if they try to hold her. It is embarrassing! Still, it doesn't bother THEM: they are so intrigued by the white baby. They are also awed by Meg and Anne. They tell the girls, "You are so beautiful," and want to touch their hair. I guess blonde hair is novel.

July 24, 1992:

Yesterday, Doreen, Becca, and I took the guard, Henry, with us to downtown Lusaka on the minibus. I now know that whites do not generally ride the minibus and why! We spent three hours on foot, checking out the shops and "State Stores" to see what was available. NOT MUCH! We also went to the market—a city block of filth, food, flies, and first-hand bartering. Smells were pungent or rancid, take your pick. It was novel and educational the first time through, but I'll gladly let the men shop for me.

I had Rebecca with me in my arms the entire time. She makes quite a spectacle. Everyone, men included, stop what they are doing to see her, point, and say "bay-bay." Henry says they rarely see white babies, especially in the market. Glad I took her. If it hadn't been for Rebecca, we wouldn't have been able to get onto the minibus to come home. We hit rush hour, and you have to FIGHT, literally, to get on the bus: visualize elbows and passengers crushing each other in a plunge for limited seats. The conductor saw Henry carrying the Umbroller, and me with the baby. He let Henry pay him to give us a seat. They put us in the FRONT, next to the driver where I could watch all the maniac driving. The art of minibus maneuvers is a balance of speed and pot-hole dodging. Throw caution to the wind. If there are speed limits, they are definitely unenforced. I had a few silent heart attacks, while Rebecca fell asleep in my arms. I decided this ride was the perfect activity for American Junior High Youth groups—an adult version of bumper cars.

Today, after putting Rebecca down for a nap, Doreen and I launched out again, this time for the American Embassy, and this time, Doreen arranged for a taxi. Soon a grass green car pulled into the gate and the driver motioned for us to get into the back seat. Doreen opened her side, and I mine. Both of us sat down simultaneously, and instantly rolled to the center with a gentle bump and "oohph!." The springs in the back seat were fully shot. Doreen's eyes twinkled with amusement. We both kept quiet about the missing parts as we readjusted ourselves on the sunken, lumpy cushion. Doreen sat nicely in a "bottom hole," obviously used by others; I chose to sit on the front edge, where there was some sense of firmness. We each braced ourselves for the open road and another adventure!

Because I'd always loved variety and the stimulation of new things, I didn't realize the symptoms of culture shock. Our trip to the American Embassy revealed how much I missed the familiarity of my own homeland. When we arrived at the gate, I saw my own country's flag and that Marine standing at attention. I just gawked. I couldn't believe I was wishing he would speak to me, to say something that sounded familiar. Once inside the building, I stared at my own president's picture; other real, live Americans; the flag; and the other marine guarding the door.

I told Doreen excitedly, "Look! It's an American! It SOUNDS like

America in here!" I savored the sound of Americanese being spoken and lustily drank in the sights of my countrymen.

She laughed heartily at me, "You've got it bad, Rachel!"

"Got what?"

"Culture shock."

I had no idea of my symptoms.

The consulate met us cordially. Hearing that we were registering as new arrivals in the country, he connected us with groups of social interest: the American/Canadian Women's Club, The Lusaka Music Society, and others. I inquired about a piano teacher for Megan and possible pianos for sale. He directed us to a board with postings of goods for sale.

Looking over the board, I had an adrenaline rush. "Ha! Look at that!" Then my face fell. "It's about $1,500! Forget that!" I told Doreen. "I'm just going to ask **God** for a piano and **wait**. God can feed a million Israelites in total wilderness, and He can provide us with a piano in Lusaka. If it's not His will, I will learn to be happy without one." I announced this with conviction so I would listen to myself. We had a nasal-sounding keyboard that we'd brought over on the container, but I knew it was inadequate for Megan's developing technique. I really believed we needed a *piano*.

The return trip to the Bell's home was another ride through this surreal experience of Africa. I enjoyed watching it, like a new movie that had no ending. The streets, potholes, people, businesses, uniformed school children, and people interacting with each other were scenes I watched with rapt attention. Everything was novel and intriguing, a wonder to me and a study in "Future Life."

We pulled into the Bell's gate, "home" again. Actually, it did not feel exactly like home to me, though, because Jim was not there. On the other hand, it was a place of familiarity and friendliness. I was getting to know my new co-workers; the children were happy; I had every-thing essential. This overstuffed place was a wonderful launching pad for relationships and explorations into the unknown. It was a refuge, a place of comfort and comradery during the transitions into another life. To this day, I am thankful for the hospitable spirit of Steve and Ruth Ann's family, my first "home" in Zambia.

Our Zambia Missionary Team

Chapter 10

The New Normal

When the men returned from South Africa with vehicles, appliances, and supplies, the place exploded with excited bedlam: dogs barking; kids screaming their pleasure; wives rushing to their husbands. We had not heard from the men or Sherry in weeks, so our quiet anxieties regarding their welfare were instantly relieved when the first car entered the yard. All were exceptionally weary, and nerves were a bit frayed from three days of pushing to meet border closings and beat nightfall. To finally be home and see family was emotional release, even for the men. At last the new definition of "normal" could emerge from life in Africa.

In the next weeks, each family began the search for their own homes. The property proposal at Buckley Estates had fallen through. The owner reneged on the agreed rental price, and the team determined the location was not strategic for outreach anyway. It was just as well, in our thinking, to get the salt out of the shaker and into the African world, rather than clumped together in one location. Meanwhile, living in a house with twenty one occupants held interesting activities.

August 7, 1992:

Everyday living is quite a chore in Africa. I've found nothing in my repertoire from the USA to compare to it. Well, maybe camping in Mohican State Park, "primitive area B" is close. I can tell this will be good for me, as it surely will strengthen my perseverance muscle, that is, if I don't pull a hamstring every time we lose the convenience of electricity or water! Those are two commodities I depend on to accomplish my goals, so losing them frequently is a strain on my patience!

I've been getting up at 5:30 every morning to do wash, as it gives me the illusion that I'm getting ahead. Besides that, I have a chance of using the one washing machine for at least an hour. Electricity is strong enough at that time to spin dry the hand-washed clothes, of which I have plenty. The hot water heater (called a "geyser" here) also does not work much at this brown-out level. This morning I washed my hair in cold water and amused myself thinking about Monday's wash. I began washing with determination and prayer, and practiced my newly acquired discipline: singing. When I wasn't singing, I was having mental conversations with myself. I finished scrubbing about noon with a sense of victory, a dread for tomorrow's wash and sore knuckles. There is no way to escape dirt here or laundry for eight. I AM adjusting—a little begrudgingly, I admit. Larry reminds me that it really is overwhelming to face life African style the first time particularly when adding ministry, a big family, and culture to the mix. Did I forget to mention dogs? There are five, barking dogs—plus protective OWNERS to contribute to my "new culture." But the Lord brings His word to mind and consoles my frustrations.

While adjustments were not initially comfortable, I wrote down what I DID like, even prefer over the United States. It helped to keep "change" positive:

1. Zambians take time for hospitality and relationships.

2. They aren't astounded by large families. (Yeah for us!)

3. They are hungry to learn.

4. They are profoundly polite and sensitive; very accepting.

5. We are NEVER late in this culture!

6. They take everything in stride.

Uh, there are positives and negatives to that. The positives are that they don't panic or even complain about only two or three days of water per week. They just use it when it's there, and find some way to store or haul it when it's turned off. Americans would be having a fit. I know!

The same thing goes for the telephone and electricity service. The Bell's phone hasn't worked since we arrived! There are so few hours when electricity is strong enough to turn on the computers and labor-saving devices. Still, the Zambians shrug and wait for tomorrow. I can't yet get beyond my American "value" that accomplishing my to-do list is important. I can feel like such a loser, and I don't like it!

The negative side to complacency is just as astounding to me. For example, we went house hunting in a pleasant, upscale neighborhood. In the new houses, nothing is square or plumb and everything has paint droppings on it. Ok, so Zambians don't use drop cloths, and it doesn't matter to them! Culture shock for us perfectionists has high voltage.

Easing into Africa as a group was consoling for me; it was a cushion for a softer landing into the ministry. However, I kept waiting for someone to tell me how to do this job. There was no real occupational training for all these cultural and personal adjustments, not to mention that there was no structure to the day. Jim was accustomed to a job with regular hours and set tasks. I was used to managing the house and children. It gave purpose, accomplishment and definition to the day. No one explained what the "missionary day" was supposed to look like or to accomplish. It seemed like we were expected to figure everything out by the barefoot method...trial and error. We asked the veteran missionaries about culture and expectations, but some of their answers only revealed that they had their own uncomfortable adjustments to make. We were all new to this particular country and its idiosyncrasies. No one was an expert yet. Still, we were the only ones with no cross-cultural experience in ministry. Living closely—very closely—as a team was probably one of God's ways of forcing the mentoring process.

Six weeks of twenty-one people in one house had convinced us that togetherness was only good to a point. It appeared that everyone had reached The Point. One Zambian man said to me, "We Africans are watching you whites. If it had been twenty-one of us living in one house, we would have killed each other by now." Then he noted, "But you all seem to like each other." That was encouraging, but the house-hunting intensified. The Bells persevered in sharing their home willingly, despite the fact that they longed for privacy too.

For us, the real estate options were depressing. We were the biggest family on the tightest budget. While the rest of the team was settling into their homes, they continued praying, looking, and encouraging us. Larry and Jim decided to check with the Southern Baptists, as they had a large missionary presence in the city. One of their mission homes was vacant for six months, while their missionaries were stateside on furlough. The price was fair to market value ($800/month), but our budget dictated a maximum of $500 per month. We needed the house; they needed the occupancy, so God gave a spirit of brotherhood and cooperation between us. Larry, like a protective, big brother, mediated a deal for us, and we moved in immediately.

What a relief to have a house that had been designed for American occupants. It had laundry hookups, kitchen cupboards, electric wall plugs, and spacious rooms. The great room had built-in bookshelves and a beautiful, parquet floor. The house made it easy to feel at home, even though we lacked furniture to fill it. We bought grass-woven chairs and love seat from the side of the road, and used the Bell's ping-pong table for eating. Seven plastic chairs, seven beds and a port-a-crib, a desk left by the mission, and a few wall hangings from the C.A.R. shipment completed our first furnishings. Anne hand painted a cardboard heart which hung on the wall, "Home is where you hang your heart."

While the house was scantly furnished, it was an easy transition for our African home. A greater adjustment was learning to accept predictable unpredictability, such as the mail system, electricity, water, security, and phone service, to name a few examples. Jim wrote, "I guess the mail around here works the same way the phone system does... it's kind of a roulette game. As you dial the number, the ball is started. If it falls into the right slot, the call connects. Otherwise you get a busy signal and have to try again … and again … and again. Don't take me wrong, we are very thankful to have a phone system at all, but it makes life kind of comical. Excuse me … the phone is ringing … Ok … that was a short call—an occurrence that happens rather frequently. The phone company's roulette ball must have fallen into someone else's slot (call truncated). I guess that's their way of teaching their customers to keep it short."

The longer we lived in the context of undependability, the more the novelty and sense of adventure wore thin, replacing humor with feelings of stress. Africans were very pragmatic about their lives and habits. Some of their mannerisms were definite taboos to our way of thinking: men urinating in public, cleaning out one's nose without tissues, holding hands between same gender friends. On the other hand, some of our lifestyle was just as offensive to their sense of propriety: open displays of affection between genders; not giving a lift to anyone on the street; our habits of privacy, personal space, and ownership. Some days we handled the frustration with grace. Other days, we cried out for mercy: the aggravations brought out our weaknesses. The learning curve was so steep at times that it threatened to pitch us off.

Gradually, I was getting accustomed to places, people, procedures, and common problems. Our perspective was often kept intact by writing it all down to share with those who would understand our struggles and intrigues. The simplest things, like communicating or shopping or eating or going to town, became a reason to stare or to laugh or to puzzle us.

In August 1992, I wrote:

I noticed as we drove through Lusaka today that I was not gawking at all the sights. That's a good sign that I am getting accustomed to SOME things, and now consider normal what was once novel.

You only have to be here one day to realize there are very few ordinances enforced in Lusaka. You can burn freely, litter freely, ignore red lights after dusk, and never wear seatbelts IF your car has them.

They can wear ANY combination of clothes. Some guys even wear outdated women's clothing from the USA, unknowingly, of course: tops, hats, coats, sports clothes. I saw this athletic dude swaggering down the street, cocky and strutting, wearing a high school varsity jacket from the US. Fascinating thing was it was a cheerleader's jacket, with the megaphone "letter" and "Cheryl" written on it. He had no clue how not-cool it was.

After finding a parking space and paying a guard boy to watch our car, we leave for the department store which boasts a fashion-center on the second floor. As we walk up the broken escalator, we're sure we are back in a second-hand shop the day after Christmas rush. Clothing on the racks is dingy, soiled, or terribly outdated—take your pick. Several of the sweaters have hangers poking through the shoulders. The floor badly needs to be mopped. African rumbas are playing loudly from "The Modern Music Center" made of outdated LP records and cassettes. All ads and prices are handwritten with magic marker on typing paper. Hmmm. Not what I expected from a fashion center.

Want to try the furniture store? The biggest one has stock that consists of 1960's era living-room sofas and chairs. Dining-room sets look OK from fifty-feet away, and bedroom furniture completely lacks enticement. Everyone accepts furniture with what we consider imperfect blemishes, stains, smudges, scrapes and gouges. These are not big deals to them.

Across the boulevard, you might enjoy the supermarket, where a few US manufacturers have products displayed on handmade, wooden shelves: Johnson & Johnson, Ivory, Colgate. Milk comes in pint bags and is usually sour by the time you get it home. We buy direct from the dairy farm, taking twenty-liter buckets to fill. I have to pasteurize and "homogenize" it myself. Big mess. There is more variety if one is willing to pay the price: several kinds of cereal, jams, cookies, Coke, and soaps. We buy our meat at the butcher's and our eggs elsewhere. I guess I'd better move on. I sense Kroger and the American malls calling....

Some of you asked about our food. We're eating a combination of African and American. The first month we ate a lot of African nshima and sauces (relishes), but since we are now on our own, I've treated the family to some of the canned goods and mixes that transferred here from our C.A.R. shipment, that is, whatever the rats did not devour. They apparently feasted on several pounds of our M&M's, chewing gum, filet of rugs, lampshades au jus, and eggshell-mattress custard. The kids found a box of untouched Rice Krispies and two-year old puffed wheat. They thought they were great—albeit, slightly stale.

September, 1992:

Lusaka is such a blend of traditional Africans trying to live in the modern world. As you drive to the center of town, you're following one of many "carriage buses," with its billowing, black cloud of pollution. Cars, MOST of which show signs of former accidents, are jerking around each other, honking. I can see I will need to change my former, "nice" driving habits. Here it's drive to survive, whatever that takes for those of us who were not born with kamikaze genes.

Today I drove into town, sweaty palms and all. I kept whispering to myself, "Think left, think left." Cars drive on the left hand side of the road in Zambia. A few times I attempted to shift the doorknob on my right instead of the stick shift on my left. I also practiced swerving, dodging maniacs, horn blowing, and various jerky manip-ulations which seem to indicate a "seasoned driver." I'm really beginning to fit into the culture! You just have to pretend you're in a whole city of Driver's Ed students who use speed as the way to show they are skilled. Actually, in my case, the white knuckles, clenched teeth, and wide-eyed peepers are a dead giveaway that I do NOT feel "seasoned" here.

Well, with that in mind, would you pray for me as I go for my Zambian driver's license: there are NO manuals available for us to study laws and road signs. Steve asked the road traffic control department for anything that might help us prepare for the test. They gave him one paper with the explanation of the road signs and required him to return it after we'd all shared it! This is definitely third-world class living.

We did get our licenses, thanks to Steve. He convinced the road officers that our driving experience and training in America was more than adequate for driving here. They allowed us to waive the road test, and we only took the written exam over signs and laws. When we finished, I felt like a victorious Junior Higher who had just been granted her go-cart license.

Once we had completed many of the business essentials for residency, we were free to focus on other interests. Several of us had window shopped the Lusaka options for furnishings and longed to expand our options. During the national trade show in August, we saw beautiful tables on display from a Swedish trade school in the Eastern Province. Several from the team were ready for an outing, so we packed lunches and ourselves into Larry's van in hopes of seeing Zambia and some great made-to-order furniture.

The trip took about four hours one way, through mountains and points of interest. Our translator, Lungu, told us that there was a landmark hot springs about an hour from the capital. We were all in the mood for some excitement, so we began to anticipate the tourist spot, and maybe even an international eatery. I kept looking for signs of the place, some evidence of a developed gathering place. If Lungu had not announced that we were "*there*," I would never have known we'd just passed The Place of Interest! *There* was a bare spot beside the road and a grassy path to the springs. *There* in the water were women and children bathing and washing their clothes. This was The Real Africa, natural and pragmatic, not defiled by commercialism or people gazers (other than ourselves). We walked to the water's edge to feel its warmth—like tepid bath water—and then traced the stream to the spring's source. Here, it created steam in the morning air. The scenes of huts and Zambians bathing among the reeds made my adrenaline pump with excitement. Now this *felt* like the Africa I'd imagined.

I did not realize exactly how natural Africa felt until we were back in the car and I experienced a "nature call." I'd been looking for a roadside rest, but kilometer after kilometer recycled the same scenery: potholes, bush country, huts, and Africans. I whispered to Jim to suggest that we stop for a break. He did. Larry pulled over and announced, "Women to the left; men to the right!" I looked at Jim with wide eyes. We were in the middle of nowhere. My face probably showed my sense of lostness in this "art of bush living." Everyone scattered to find privacy in the foliage, so I followed their lead, totally petrified of snakes, wild animals, and some man coming out from behind a tree unaware. Doreen or Sallie, seeing my face, stood guard several yards away. This was today's reality check on "natural living!"

Once we arrived at our destination, the town of Petauke, we discovered another reality. You can drive for hours, only to arrive at a lot of nothing. Yes, there was a training school there. It amounted to a pile of planks and a crude building, but no supervisors were present. No, there were no samples to look at. Yes, they would be willing to make something on order, but we had to accept it sight unseen. Ok, so much for that four-hour drive. We stretched our legs, took contact numbers, and turned around for Lusaka.

Everyone was hungry, but lunch was mostly gone. We all pooled our leftovers, and then stopped at a "Take Away," an African version of fast food. We ordered boiled eggs and samosas, a deep-fried, meat-filled dumpling-of-sorts. We tried to get fresh water, but had to settle for chugging down our orange Fantas before leaving. You were not allowed to take the bottles unless you paid extra. We returned to the city after dark, somewhat sick from tainted samosas. Very thirsty and thoroughly tired from road wear, we felt like we had accomplished next to nothing in fulfilling the day's goals—getting furniture. I was to learn in the next months, how normal this feeling is. Accomplishment in Africa is not often measured by setting or reaching goals or having completed a to-do list. There was another standard for progress, and we had yet to discover it.

Chapter 11

And Just Who Is My Neighbor?

Adjusting to culture was one thing. It involved change in what we *did*. Adjusting to people was even more complex; it involved *who we actually were*, and that was ever so hard to change. Once the team had dispersed, and we were on our own in a new neighborhood, we felt our vulnerability, our naivety, our exposure as Americans trying to live in Africa. We sensed more keenly how we did not yet "fit" in this place. Our ministry was to PEOPLE, not merely to a culture, and we barely knew any PEOPLE. Now, what were we going to do about it?

Jesus had said, "Love your neighbor as yourself."[1] What was that supposed to look like in this context? Back in America, I FELT loving. I enjoyed good friends, fellowship, and mutual respect. I thought I loved others; my family, my church, my friends, the lost—in a most generic way. Yet, one Scripture seemed to uncover me. "If you love those who love you, what reward have you?"[2] I was now in a context where I was yet unknown and unloved. I did not know where to begin, though I was willing to love anybody, or so I thought.

Our new, temporary home was on the corner of a busy intersection, surrounded by a cement block wall fence. Both Jim and I hated the blockade. To us, fences symbolized keeping people out, or hemming us in. However, it was culturally accepted, and there was no choice but to submit to it. We were now in a setting where crime and safety were just as much a factor as building relationships. That meant we had to "love our neighbors" behind protective walls. To add to the oxymoron, we had to get guard dogs—two German Shepherds named Okey and Yoko. They were our alarm system every time someone knocked on the gate or entered the yard. Jim wrote about them in a letter to home:

They seem to be a good deterrent to any who might venture to steal from the property. We have to tie one of them up at the gate though; he is very jealous. The other day we were giving the more congenial one a bath, while the other one stood nearby and watched. He got upset and turned on Micah, and bit him in his thigh, leaving him with a hole in his leg. The end result was that three of us had sore legs. I kicked the dog in HIS leg to get him away from Micah. When I did, I evidently wrenched my own knee. When the dog was tied up, I am not sure who ended up the worst: Micah, me, or the dog!

Getting beyond the wall fence and then past the dogs, we all dug in to build relationships. There was a constant stream of visitors knocking at the gate, most of whom wanted to sell or beg, share a sad story of poverty or sickness, or request a job. My compassionate heart could not ignore the pleas or the poverty and leanness. I seemed to be constantly attending the gate, ever interrupted from my duties with the children and house.

We had no buffer for these interrupters, meaning "neighbors." The Southern Baptists had left a village man in the servant's quarters to occupy the premises, but he knew no English and could not communicate or screen visitors for us. Our only communication with Abison was hand gestures and facial expressions, each guessing what the other meant. We pointed and mimed the jobs we wanted done outside and hoped some action—the right action—would follow. With all the new responsibilities and interruptions, I knew I would have to hire inside help eventually, but I felt reluctant. Who could you trust? We valued our privacy, and yet there wasn't much of that commodity with the continual interruptions at the gate. Whomever I hired would be key to the ministry of our home and the people who visited.

The first acceptable candidate was a docile, soft-spoken young man named Pierson. He came with a written recommendation: he was honest and a willing worker, it said. He seemed harmless enough to interview, and gentle enough to be with the kids, so I decided to try him out for a month's probationary period. His English wasn't all that good, but with patience and my newly acquired body language from communicating with Abison, I could get my task list through to him. He was thorough in completing each job, but glum in demeanor. He was also the slowest moving human I had ever seen! Simple tasks and my patience were stretched to their boundaries, as he moved at the pace of a hundred-year-old tortoise. I wasn't sure if this was normal, so I endured and prayed. I really wanted to be loving, patient, and kind, but he wasn't making this very easy!

Meanwhile, the candidates for jobs continued to knock at the gate, interrupting any and every effort at the day's progress. I was feeling urgent about getting something done, as I had six children, four of whom needed to be homeschooled, and all of whom needed meals and clean clothes, and a cheerful mother. The milk needed to be pasteurized, bread to be made, vegetables bleached, and a host of other chores necessary for third-world living. I needed help, efficient help, and I prayed for God to send me someone.

One day, Pierson called me to the gate. A small, wiry man in a black leather jacket stood there, holding his reference papers and a registration card. He was asking for a job, telling me that he had a large family to feed, and would I please consider him? I began a series of inquiries about his faith, his values, his family, his work experience. He seemed a bit cocky to me, very self-assured, but definitely energetic and friendly. I could not say that for Pierson. I promised to think about it, and invited him to return the next day.

After discussing it with Jim and praying about it, we decided to also hire Mr. Banda on a probationary contract. Initially, it sounded like a good idea. However, we did not take into account the factor of African jealousy. It was a miserable two weeks. Banda (in this culture using just his last name was proper, but we had our children call him by his title) could work circles around Pierson, and always while smiling. This made Pierson's glum, unhurried disposition all the more pronounced. The children favored Banda, as did I. His English was perfect; he could translate easily; he was teachable, could cook, and do outside work. Everything seemed perfect, except one thing: he was a Jehovah's Witness. I spoke to him about our faith, salvation, and the identity of Jesus Christ. He was clearly clueless. Jim believed this was an opportunity to expose him to the Truth. We hired Banda, and compensated Pierson for his time. I never regretted it, as God had directed our decision for a purpose, even though we did not understand it at the time. Banda had a son, who would one day become like a son to us, like a brother to our children, a best friend to Megan; a playmate, and a blessing for many years.

The day Banda moved into the servant's quarters on the property, he brought with him two sons, Harrison (12) and Nashon (10). About two weeks later, he brought his eldest daughter, Maggie, and her baby. The rest of his family lived elsewhere, he said. He seemed resistant when I encouraged him to move the whole family in, stating something about how he and his wife did not stay together nicely. I had no idea what that meant, but would soon discover once everyone arrived. The boys seemed bright, but not well educated. I decided to add them to my homeschooling efforts until they could be enrolled in the local school. Though they were considerably older than Micah, they could not read. We shared books and phonetic cards, snacks and our family classroom. The boys' favorite subject was recess, where running and climbing trees showed off their real talents. It was considerably less lonely for Micah now, and Harrison and Megan clicked immediately.

Less than a month later, Harrison turned thirteen. I made him a chocolate cake on his birthday, decorated with candles and his name and age in icing. He was so overwhelmed with gratitude. His eyes glowed in the light of the candles as we sang "Happy Birthday dear Harrison, Happy Birthday to you!" This was his first-ever birthday cake. When he and his family left the house that night, Harrison said

"Thank you very much! Thank you very much!" all the way out the door and into the darkness.

With Banda and his family on the property, we had our hands full of neighbors, all inside our wall fence. However, the "other neighbors" —the beggars and sellers and storytellers continued to come. I could now send Banda to screen the callers. Even then, both Jim and I were continually interrupted with compassion needs. Once the word got out that we cared and we gave, the requests only increased. I was personally staggering in the light of so much demand and need, plus feeling pressure from Jim, who was trying to get realistic about our resources. We even had "neighbors" when we were traveling in the car: street beggars and street children came up to the car, always with pitiful expressions and their hands out. They seemed intent on extracting something from your heart and purse. There was no escape, and I just didn't have enough "love" to go around!

At the same time, we had begun youth ministry in all three church starts. This was even more exposure to new "neighbors"—and to more need. Steve pastored two of the church starts, and Larry the third. All had disadvantaged people, but Larry's work in Chawama was in a shanty compound. Here, the unemployed, orphans and widows, sick and destitute, and common laborers multiplied exponentially. The main road into the community was a sight that took my breath away. The potholed road was surrounded by streams of people, similar to moving colonies of ants. The neighborhood was high-density housing —mostly cement block homes the size and shape of sheds—surrounded by stick, grass, or block-wall fences. Small shops, booths, and markets were interspersed between the houses along the road—people trying to eek out a living from others who had little to nothing. This place took my heart to new dimensions. I did not know how to respond, where to begin, how to view my limitations. In a letter to my parents I witnessed what my eyes and heart were seeing:

Ministry here seems overwhelming: so great a need; such openness
to hear; such eagerness to learn anything that we are willing to teach!

Poverty continues to jolt me. This week I read Jesus' words, "For I was hungry and you gave me food…I was naked, and you clothed me…inasmuch as you did it to one of the least of these My brethren, you did it to Me."³ This was too much! I laid my head on my hands and bawled and bawled. The church people are poorer than I have ever had to live with. People at Westside, an inner-city church where my dad had pastored were poor, but they had welfare as a back-up. These people just do without.

Thursday, I spent the evening trying to hold together Abison's trousers. They are embarrassingly exposing. After machine-stitching every single seam in them, and doing three iron-on patches on the seat, I pressed and returned them. He only owns two pair of pants, both of which are in tatters. The next morning, he was still wearing his dirty grey ones instead of the repaired one. I said, "Abison, where are the trousers I fixed?" He imitated trying to button, and squeezing into them. They didn't fit anymore because the seams were all sewed shut! It was true! So last night I promised to move the button over.

Giving is more than just money and materials. We are giving ourselves like never before. We have to make a decision about ministry…and how much we can handle. We're already working with both congregations to do all the music and youth, plus Larry asked us to do the new convert's discipleship class, and we've already got Bible study and counseling going elsewhere. I've opened a sewing class and Bible study with Maggie and friends, and Jim is mentoring and building a relationship with Weston, a young man needing to learn carpentry skills. Our first youth meetings are just beginning in two churches as well, and that means more relationships are developing. "Neighbors" and the gate are extremely time and energy consumptive.

The "gate neighbors" had a particularly draining effect on me. After listening to heartbreaking stories of hunger and loss, deprivation, and sickness, I was losing steam quickly. I tried to give everyone something, driving myself with "in that you have done it unto the least of these… ye have done it unto me."⁴ I told myself I could not turn Jesus away at the gate. It was my inexperience, sincerity, and lack of knowledge of the Word that caused me to respond this way. And this is how God kindly taught me a lesson.

One day I was called to the gate. The man said he was a truck driver, stranded without food or money. He needed oil for his transmission. He promised that as soon as he got his load delivered, he would bring us a large bag of rice in appreciation for our assistance. I passed the scenario on to Jim, and we decided to give him food and money for oil. Remembering the verse about treating others as if they were Jesus, I pulled out a nice cut of beef, some milk, and other foods and handed it through the gate. Then I told him my husband had added money for the needed oil, explaining that we were Christians and that this was being done in respect of Jesus. The look on the man's face was astonishment. He was a volley of accolades and promises of rice as soon as he got the truck going.

Days passed, and the driver never showed up with rice. I was feeling "taken," drained emotionally and financially from other beggars, more stories, more giving and limited resources. I was no longer giving cheerfully the way God does. I felt like the whole society was extracting something right out of my very soul.

Three weeks later, Banda called me to the gate again, this time with a smirk on his face. There was the truck driver. After exchanging greetings, I decided to test him. "Oh! You're back! How was your trip? Did you bring some rice?" Subconsciously, I felt like there ought to be a payback with all this giving, even though I didn't want to acknowledge it. A long story followed. The truck had a broken part and on and on. I was not moved. He begged. He pleaded for money and help. My skepticism grew. I called for Jim to take care of him. Jim gave him money for the part and told him that if it didn't work, we would not give anymore. The man again volleyed out the accolades and promises to return with rice. It was just a verbal bribe.

Meanwhile, we were up to our necks in "neighbors." After having a pep-talk on family togetherness and the importance of marriage with

Banda, he had unenthusiastically called his wife and the rest of the children to live with him and the boys on the property. With two large families sharing an enclosed half-acre, the noise levels increased a few decibels. However, it was the night sessions that drained us most. The marriage had unresolved conflicts and unrestrained anger. Long hours of counseling only seemed effective until they left our house; then Mrs. Banda would return to obsessive and often violent behavior. It was tearing the family apart, not restoring them. Our own family was feeling the strain as well. No matter how much I gave to "fix" the problem, it didn't "fix."

It was into this scenario, that the truck driver again reappeared. This time there was a long and different story. I listened, knowing this was another set-up. I reminded him my husband had already stated that we had helped all we could. He did not give up. The story grew; the pleadings intensified. He seemed to think he had a real cow to milk here, and it wasn't yet dry. I called Jim and walked back toward the house at Pierson's tortoise pace, leaving Jim to decide. My heart was so heavy. I looked wide-eyed into the sky and prayed audibly, "God? How do You do this? How do You give to people every day, over and over, when they never appreciate You? They just keep using You. How do you allow the rain to fall on the just AND the unjust? Do You ever get tired of us?" I made it to my room before an emotional dam burst. I felt so inadequate to represent a generous and loving God. What was I doing here?! I didn't feel like Him at all. In fact, every effort to imitate Christ's love only seemed to accentuate how little I *could* imitate it.

When I finally cried myself out, I opened my Bible to check on that passage I'd read recently. "Give to him who asks you, and from him who wants to borrow from you do not turn away. You have heard that it was said, 'You shall love your neighbor and hate your enemy.' But I say to you, 'Love your enemies and pray for those who persecute you, that you may be sons of your Father in heaven. He makes His sun to rise on the evil and on the good, and sends rain on the just and on the unjust. For if you love those who love you, what reward have you?...

Therefore you shall be perfect, just as your Father in heaven is perfect."[5] There was no way to love perfectly and completely with all these people plus my own family. I couldn't do it. No way.

Whether it was the people at the gate, the disturbed and disturbing, the diseased, the abused, the dying, the annoying... these were my new neighbors. I was to be Christ to them. I found a terrible truth. I was not worthy to be here. I did not love like He does. I was inadequate, short-sighted, lacking His kind of generosity and mercy. I hated being ripped off, lied to, and laughed at when I tried to do the right thing culturally, or to speak their language.

By the sweet provision of my Savior, I picked up the book, *Kept For the Master's Use* by Francis Ridley Havergal. It spoke directly to my need, and led me to a weeping confession—quite needed. I'd been losing joy, like a balloon leaking air or a lifeboat sinking, knowing something was not going right, but groping to identify it. The mere recognition of my personal inadequacy before God must have been what He was looking for. A sweet bliss replaced the spot where my troubled broodings had been.

The kind of love God wanted from me could only be produced by divine importation. It was a by-product—a fruit, not just a deed— that is produced when one's roots are embedded in the very Spirit of Jesus Christ. It could only be sustained as I responded to that Spirit. A blanket command to cover equal giving to everyone simply would not work. It ran out when fatigue, human emotion, and resources ran dry. But God... God WAS love, and real love *never* fails.

Chapter 12

Lessons

It was fall on the calendar, but the weather was not what enticed us towards fresh books, new pencils, and bright classrooms. It was hot, hot enough to melt initiative for anything but a pool! Regardless, the children began school the end of September with the other MKs at the Fogles' house, twenty minutes across town. Larry donated much of the funding and Jim, the labor, to convert and furnish their carport into a decent schoolroom for the kids. A retired, elementary school teacher, Tobie Worley, flew in from the States to join Sherry Segal, who was supervising the high school courses. We had chosen to supplement Calvert and University of Nebraska distance learning so that we could benefit from the transcripts and accountability offered. Even with these tools, we began to experience the tremendous balancing act between schooling children and initiating a new ministry in a foreign culture. It was no small issue, and it was no small sacrifice on anyone's part. Thankfully, we teamed up for the task: Sherry sacrificed her own ministry goals for the kids' sake; Larry, Sallie, and Tobie invested precious time; and I taught Micah, Harrison, and Nashon at home, along with the little ones.

While everyone was not behind a desk, we were all in school. Mary and Becca were enrolled in "Fundamentals of Growth," where most was learned by the barefoot method, trial and error, that is. Becca was into "Elemental Entomology." The threat of insects sent her into hyper-brain alert. Naturally, we professors taught by example and lecture, but she clearly did not take note. The sight of any bug, small or ominous, ugly or cute, even a piece of lint that resembled one sent Rebecca into hysterics. In her panic her cry would force out all her air until her diaphragm locked in place and, then she would pass out for lack of oxygen; seconds later, after her diaphragm relaxed, she could inhale and then regain consciousness, at which point she was slightly more teachable. Living in "Insect Paradise" was like having class in the "Place of Torment." Oh, the lessons we all had in helping her overcome fears!

Mary, on the other hand, had very few reservations about bugs, people, or anything else. She could throw her weight around on critters or people. Her specialty: taking charge. One day, Jim overheard her instructing Banda, "WHAT are YOU DOING?" Jim stopped her in her tracks, called her over, and expressed his displeasure at her rudeness. He let her know that if she needed to know something, she could *ask politely.* So, she turned around and approached Banda again, this time with a sugary voice, "I would like to know" (pause to think what Daddy had said and to take a deep breath) "just what it is that you are up to!" Jim and Banda, professors for a day, lost all composure!

Mary specialized in her kitchen lab. As I worked on supper, she would create her own "potted water" or special goops. One night she brought her most recent entrée to the table. Everyone oohed and ahhed as she dished out samples of her creation to brave takers: coconut, milk, barley, oats, water, flour, and other secret ingredients. Then she sat down to enjoy her culinary arts. In the next scene, Mary's spoon hit the floor. She began sputtering and spewing out coconut pieces and the mixture, wailing as she grappled for her glass of water, "It's yucky, Mommy! It's yucky!" Mary learned lessons best with self-discovery.

Jim and I were also in a self-discovery mode. One day Jim went to town to purchase materials from the hardware store. He went to the counter and began his business request just like he would in the States. "I'd like..." and completed his list. The man looked as if he were deaf. Jim began to enunciate clearer, in case lip reading was necessary.

Rather unexpectedly, the clerk enunciated in return, "Hello! How are you?" Jim stopped, looked blank, and then realized his error. He should not "open" any conversation until the greetings, "How are you?" had been exchanged. Anything less was discourteous. His day's lesson: business second; relationships first.

The Nyanja language was another barefoot subject for the family. Nathan learned his on the soccer field. Megan and Harrison swapped words while perched atop the wall fence or in the playhouse. The Banda family on the property was excellent for teaching and translating for everyone, though our forgetters triggered more easily than our retainers. The team did find a fifteen-lesson language course and a German anthropologist coach the following year. Meanwhile, we did try to keep a small, working vocabulary in use throughout each day. The people were much more responsive when we at least tried their language and ways.

One very intriguing subject in our barefoot school was body language. I was discovering that the Zambians had a whole dictionary of signals and gestures, all of which meant something; none of which were explained except by interpreters. One afternoon we hosted a meal for Lungu, one of the key leaders we were grooming for the youth program at Chawama. I asked him a yes-no question, did he want such and such? He looked straight at me and raised his eyebrows, almost like he was surprised. I thought my question had startled him, so I asked him a second time. Again, he raised his eyebrows, but not with any verbal response. Was my question inappropriate? A third time, I repeated the inquiry, this time right in his face. Lungu's eyebrows raised as high as he could stretch them in exaggeration. Were it not for his lids holding in the eyeballs, they would have fallen onto the table.

"Lungu? Does raising your eyebrows mean yes?"

Lungu threw his head back and laughed out an explanation. In body language, he had been "shouting" yes!

We were all learning something fun every single day: music, sports, and family recreation. Megan began piano lessons with Mrs. Hoskins, a British piano teacher whose husband conducted the Lusaka Chamber Orchestra where Anne and I played once a week. The three eldest children took swimming lessons at the pool a few blocks from the house, and Jim coached Anne and a couple other girls, in running at a local school track. When we lacked ideas for our Tuesday family day, we learned to improvise: flashlight tag in the dark, roasting marshmallows at the trash pile, chasing blue-head lizards, telling jokes on ourselves about our cultural bloopers. We could even find amusement as we adjusted to accepted social etiquette in this place—albeit definite no-no's for own sense of manners: picking one's nose, urinating without privacy, hand holding between same gender friends, mothers' breastfeeding in every conceivable position or place. Culture shock could actually add some merriment to our school in Zambia.

Some of the workbook exercises of Zambia were not as enjoyable. The traditions and practices brought some consternation as we tried to understand and interpret them through the light of Scripture. Traditions associated with marriage were quite shocking for those of us who had no prior exposure or working experience. Our counseling relationships with a few couples gave us a raw look at the common marital issues, and serious concerns over the structure and expectations of marriage in this culture. Problems recycled over unpaid dowries, which partner has authority in the family, when the marriage begins, extended-family live-ins, and many financial and control issues. While we were educated in Biblical knowledge, the application of those principles was challenging to sort out in another cultural setting. Sometimes, we flunked in understanding, and had to do more research in Wisdom. This was definitely an upper level course which extended into the Master's level.

One required track for our Zambian education was terribly difficult: our indoctrination into pandemic death. At that time, Lusaka held the highest death rate per capita in the world. We could not absorb all the material and experiences at once, as it was crushing to the soul. I could no longer sing that pew-song from childhood, "Rescue the perishing;

care for the dying. Snatch them in pity from sin and the grave. Weep … lift up … tell them of Jesus….” I simply could not get through the song without choking up. I wrote in my lessons: “There's too much perishing here; too many graves, and an endless stream of erring ones to weep over and I do! I am continually thankful to be here, but it hurts my soul to see what we see.”

By Thanksgiving, we had graduated from novice to beginner status. While it seemed like we had accumulated some knowledge, we had only learned how much there was yet to be taught. We were Pilgrims in a new land. God had given us some Squantos and Pocahontases this year to help us through, so we had much to celebrate that first Thanksgiving. Our team gathered at the Fogle's around roasted chickens and a festive spread. Levity and our own American traditions satisfied our temporary wants, along with watching VHS tapes of the Olympics that had just arrived in the mail. We were grateful that year, more than other years, because we finally realized what we have. The Spirit of God was teaching us in a classroom where deep poverty and death opened our eyes and hearts at last to the life and wealth we already had in the Lord's blessings.

* * *

“Bless the Lord, O my soul, and forget not all his benefits.”[1]

Chapter 13

A Tea Party for Aliens

The weekly trips to the Chawama church plant were like excursions to another planet, as far as our connectedness went. We all had sincere desires to relate to these people, and loved them with fascination, but frankly, we were aliens to them, and they to us. Simply put, our lifestyles had little in common. I longed to get past the starry-eyed view of one another and defy the gravity that pinned us to our own planets. I wanted out of our VW spaceship as we zoomed past the shacks and the people each week. I longed to bring them into my world, just do **something** that would bridge this distance between our lives.

Our friend Byron told us, "You will always find you have more in common with others than differences. Look for the commonalities." Remembering that, I discovered one interesting link: we both loved tea, and being women, we loved to get out. An idea began to form as Christmas season drew near. I wanted to host a tea party at my house, give them my very best, and then in the devotional time would present the Lord Jesus. It seemed like a perfect bridge. I shared my heart with Sallie and she was willing to team up with me, provided Larry was willing to help Jim with transporting women both ways. It was a major undertaking to get women twenty-five minutes across town. Larry and Jim agreed to help, and the invitation was announced at church. The usually silent "sitters" took note, leaning forward on their benches with interest. We heard there was no small stir in the compound, as the women planned and borrowed what they would wear to the Christmas tea. At last we had stepped onto common turf.

Sallie and I set to work making sheet cakes and decorating cookies. I pulled out the Christmas tree and manger scene so that they could see some of our Western traditions for celebrating the holidays. I also prepared the devotional on God's gift to us—eternal life through His own Son, and how to receive it.

The day of the tea party I was excited. I put out my very best: the green linen table cloth, trays and platters of cookies, teas from my own stash, Christmas napkins, and all my cups and mugs. I put on a Christmas tape and finished setting out every possible chair we owned. Sallie came early, bringing her tea pot, baked goods, and more plastic chairs. We finished all the preparations and just waited for our guests to arrive.

It was now beyond the intended starting time, so I was a bit anxious. I still had not relaxed with the fluid arrival times of the Africans: there was no "late." As Sallie and I were killing time, we heard the distinctive sound of our VW Combie engine and two choirs of women singing at the top of their lungs. I stopped talking and listened. Their sound was incredible and gorgeous and intense!

"Is THAT the women?" I asked Sallie.

The singing stopped outside our gate, and Banda ran to let them in. As the vans pulled up under the carport, the volume and enthusiasm of the women never let up. They stepped out of the vans; each carefully dressed in her very best. One woman had even purchased a black formal gown from the second-hand clothing people, and wore black, heavily scuffed pumps to complete the outfit. Their efforts to dress-up made Sallie and me look almost indifferent to the occasion! The women continued singing, dancing and whooping their cries of excitement. A shrill trill and shriek from one of the women sent a chill down my spine.

"Sallie!" I whispered, "It sounds like they are going to eat us!" I was joking, but actually sincere. If there had been a big, black caldron in the center, their cries would have been a perfect soundtrack for a scary movie. However, their faces expressed only utmost pleasure. Many of the ladies had not been out of their compound except to do business at the markets. None had been to a white woman's house. This celebration was simply a release of wild ecstasy and joy. We watched the uninhibited singing, clapping, and rhythmic dancing for about ten minutes. They were having such fun! I thought, "Oh my! What have I got myself into? We are Baptists, and they are absolutely clueless as to what Baptists think of dancing!" Sallie and I tried to get control and were ignored. We could not stop them! Finally, I ran for Banda. I asked him to invite them inside the house. Perhaps the change in setting would tame them. Gradually, they cooperated, politely removing their shoes as they entered the door.

Now it was their turn to be wide-eyed. Most had never been inside a muzungu's (white person) house, so this was like their first field trip. Some peered through the windows at the garden, the rope swing, and lawn. Some sat in the chairs and eyed the table, where piles of cakes and cookies stood waiting. Some just gazed at the Christmas tree and my décor while bouncing their babies in their chitenges to keep them pacified.

I had no idea of African protocol beyond the greeting, so I simply welcomed them all and explained how happy I was to have them in our home. While eyes were shining and smiles were genuine, I suddenly realized I was not getting through. We needed an interpreter if we to avoid returning to outer space relations.

"Does anyone here speak English?" I asked. "I need an interpreter," I repeated. Some of the women knew enough to understand my question. Heads turned to a younger woman named Joyce. I asked if she would be willing, and she simply offered with, "I can try."

Through Joyce, I again greeted the women in Nyanja and received a uniform response. Then I repeated my welcome and that I had wanted to share our American way of celebrating Christmas. I talked briefly about how we decorate a tree, how we remember the coming of Jesus to earth, and how we eat many sweets at this time. Then I explained how we would begin by going to the table, single file, taking a plate and napkin, and choosing their favorite type of tea. Joyce translated every word. We prayed, and then no one moved. I looked at Joyce.

"Did you explain what I said?" I asked.

"I did."

"Why aren't they going to the table?"

"Maybe they don't understand. I will explain it again." She did, and still no one moved. We were back in outer space, floating. Finally Sallie came over to me.

"I think they are not used to doing this the American way. They don't know what to expect." Sallie had years of experience in the Central African Republic. I trusted her. "I think *we* are supposed to serve *them*, that is what they are waiting for."

"Then let's do it!" I said.

Sallie took the lead, picking up the platters of cakes and cookies. I expected each woman to take one or two baked goods on their saucers, leaving room for their hot tea which followed. However, the women grabbed fistfuls and samples of everything that went past them. The food was piled in heaps on their plates, falling off onto the floor, or placed into their bosoms, mouths, children's hands, or wherever it would fit. I was pleased that they liked the food, but REALLY! This was NOT like American women who watch their figures and caloric intake, who like to be delicate and reserved for social graces or image. These women liked to buy up an opportunity! I was again in another world, while still in my own living room.

When we followed in the next round with tea, sugar, and milk, I was in for another adjustment. The sugar bowl which was filled, only served about three or four ladies before needing a refill, and it wasn't because the bowl was small. These women knew how to use sugar! By the time we completed our serving rounds, the ladies at the beginning of the line were looking rather sedated—sick might be a more accurate description. The heat and humidity within the room, combined with hot, sugary tea and too many sweets put everyone into a stupor.

I could tell we were losing them mentally.

"OK." I reasoned to myself. "I had these women over here because I was trying to buy up an opportunity for CHRIST! They look drunk on sugar, and what am I going to do to salvage this?" Several were slumped down in their chairs, looking hot and nauseous. That was only because they were. I was a bit annoyed that they did not seem to be equipped with self-control buttons. "What was it with this culture? It's not my fault they are sick." Rather than dealing with the situation as it was, I stuck with my own game plan: I determined to go ahead with my devotional. I may as well have been in my spaceship, for I fear I zoomed past them despite my every effort to bring them along, to make it interesting and interactive.

When I finished, some were dozing, some looked glazed. About four or five seemed to have come aboard. I asked if there were any questions about Jesus or about how to get eternal life, or anything that I deemed important. One lady raised her hand. In my heart, I was clapping. Maybe all was not in vain. Maybe one person would receive Christ as personal Savior! The woman spoke in Nyanja, and Joyce translated:

"She wants to know where the toilet is, and do you have some cold water to drink. Some of the women need fresh air."

"Oh! Of course!" I responded.

I felt bewildered and disappointed. We closed in prayer. Before I dismissed them, I handed out the hostess gift: bouillon cubes for cooking their relishes.

A soft shower of rain had cooled and refreshed the outdoors during our devotional. The wilted women—like beautiful blossoms—seemed to revive outside. I began to clear the clutter of my heart along with the dishes which lay around the room. Through the windows, I could hear the women's pleasure returning. Some were laughing and running in the yard, playing tag like children. The lady in the black formal was hanging onto the rope swing as another pushed her high into the tree limbs. Others had taken an interest in something in my garden. They were having a ball out there!

Before I could join them, one of the women came inside, asking for plastic bags. I said, "Sure! But why?" She explained there were some leaves that they wanted to take home. I was puzzled, and my face showed it. I asked again, "What do you want to use them for?"

She could not hold my gaze and giggled with a little embarrassment. After pressing the question again, she leaned over to explain her secret in my ear. Apparently something growing in my yard was used as an aphrodisiac, and these married women wanted in on it. My garden also grew something else they wanted: weeds! At least, that is what it was to me. To them, it was lunch. They said it made a nice relish. So, after getting the plastic sacks, I went outside to observe.

The women were as happy as I'd ever seen them. Ever. The bags they held in hand were filled with the leaves and blossoms of my once-beautiful bushes. Women were helping themselves to the "weeds" which I still did not value as they did. I did not understand, and I did not know how to belong to this group. I did know, however, that I was shutting down. The timing seemed appropriate for closing the afternoon's activities. Larry corralled our reluctant friends into the vans. There were sweet good-byes and waves and sighs.

I was left behind. The afternoon had not been what I'd expected, but I did not consider it to be a flop. Actually, it would be hard to measure its significance. If nothing else, I had a clearer view of the distance between our planets, and what I would need to become before I entered into a relationship in their world. As I walked back inside, a wry smile formed on my countenance. How in the world would I ever explain that my evangelistic outreach included dancing, drinking into a stupor, and a take-home pack of aphrodisiacs and weeds. I thought it might be best left a secret.

* * *

Out of Your World

Music and Lyrics by Linda R. Mohler
Used with permission

Out of Your world, You came out of Your world
To become a man, to feel and bear our sin.
Only this love could convince us all of
Your power to change the heart You live in.

You came out of Your world, out of Your world for me,
Giving Your all to buy my eternity,
What in the world could ever repay the debt I owe,
But loving the world that You came down to free.

They're so different from me, so distant from You;
But that's the way I was when You came down to me.
Only Your grace has the power to erase
The stains of my sin, and move me to be

Out of my will, and out of my world for you,
Giving my all, body and soul to be Yours.
Love through me, Christ, for You are the only Love there is
That reaches to make Your home on the distant shores.[1]

* * *

In My Dreams

Christmas is usually such a big deal. All the traditions and expectations and trappings of American celebrations were what made it "feel" like Christmas, but I hadn't realized it until we stood at the beginning of December. In 100-degree heat, I didn't "feel" like Christmas. Having no hope of family connections didn't FEEL like Christmas, either. It only highlighted the distance between us and the fresh longings for home. The December prayer letter, written on BLUE paper, began:

Ummm … Merry Christmas, I think.

*The calendar shows December and a Norman Rockwell version of Christmas, but we're having trouble believing it. The traditional feelings and anticipation of family get-togethers got a little limp in the steamy humidity and rain. So, we baked some molasses cookie cutouts and sang "Jungle Bells, Jungle Bells," feeling a little farther from home than usual. We all seem to appreciate more than we used to the Lord's **leaving His home** for earth's **far-away** place.*

That was really the Spirit of Christmas this year—leaving home. We were trying to take this holiday "spiritually," bravely, but were facing a strange clash between Ghosts of Christmases Past and the Spirit of the Present. As mother of the tribe, I purposed to make this a happy time, to try and re-create that Christmas Spirit.

Soon after Thanksgiving, we pulled out the fake Christmas tree that we'd sent over in the C.A.R. shipment. We used one of our family nights to hang decorations, drink hot chocolate, and bake cookies, all to the tunes of taped Christmas carols and traditional tunes. The old manger scene from home came out and was elevated to a focal point in the living room. I pulled out the wrapped presents we'd brought from extended family and placed them under the tree. Then I waited for the Spirit of Christmas Past to take over. Baby Jesus was in the manger; all the decorations were in place; Christmas carol tapes were playing; presents from home were under the tree; and Christmas smells from my oven wafted over the steamy house. Still, I could not resurrect the Spirit of Christmas Past, nor coax it to visit us. I actually decided maybe I wasn't supposed to have "it." The Spirit of Christmas-Yet-To-Come haunted me privately.

Somewhere in this time frame, our missionary team decided that there would be great benefits and less work for all if the three churches combined Christmas day services. Connecting the churches would encourage fellowship within the mission works, plus expand the outreach opportunities for the Gospel. These Christmas day programs are a norm, and the only big celebration of Christ's birth for the day. I volunteered to write and direct the program.

Since Christmas was about God giving His Son to us, I chose the theme: "The Perfect Gift." It never crossed my mind that Zambian Christmases would not associate Christmas with gifts. Most were too poor to give, and few ever received any gifts. Being American, I went all-out for this production: puppet presentation, songs, recitations, scheduled rehearsals *ahead of time*. I was totally clueless about the culture's carefree approach to preparing for such an event, and I was unaccustomed to tardy schedules and hit-and-miss commitment at practices. The Spirit of Christmas Practice was somewhat humbug!

Other situations in December now confronted the Spirit of Christmas Present. Our used, VW Combi Van developed engine issues—one at a time, then all at once: carburetor, rings, water pump, bearings, and seal. Routine engine repairs, greasy clothes, and sweaty trips to Soweto Market for used engine parts did little to muster a jolly season for Jim. He wrote:

Prayer is the key word for this vehicle. Because of the carburetor problems, there was serious damage done to the rings in the cylinders. This caused the vehicle to burn oil badly. That fouls the plugs, and when it does, it can use as much as three quarts of oil in a week. The parts are available, but the cost of pistons alone is over $600! I want to do what I need to, but what that is just now, I am not sure.

This dying vehicle was our sole mode of transportation and a deep frustration. The car represented more than convenience; it was our necessary escape. The Banda family's situation had become a dramatic and daily issue on our property. Something was very wrong with Mrs. Banda. It was more threatening than anyone could rightfully overlook. Counseling had not resolved the tension and turmoil in their home, so Mrs. Banda had to be taken to relatives an hour away. I now felt the responsibility to mother all eleven children on the property. I felt like the lady who lived in a shoe: so many children she didn't know what to do!

Just as my duties increased, Jim was asked to cover pastoral responsibilities for Steve Bell. Their family was leaving for a much-needed vacation break in South Africa. Jim wrote to his family:

I had the privilege of learning firsthand what it was like to be a missionary pastor for nearly three weeks. It gave me a greater appreciation for the work of a missionary who is really busy for the Lord: Steve's schedule is very hectic! Three sermons on Sundays, three Bible studies during the week, and calling on the people of two churches is enough to keep any man busy by himself. Add to these the preparations, daily chores of mail pickup, and travel from place to place to purchase necessities reminded me of the days when I ran track, you gave each race all that you could, and used every amount of breath you could possibly muster just to finish. I gained a far greater appreciation for my friends and relatives who are pastoring.

When the stress increased, Banda came down with a severe case of malaria. After treatment, he lapsed into pneumonia and was off work for three weeks. Days were filled and top-heavy with his chores. Becca was not sleeping well at night, her own case of malaria. I was the appointed angel-of-mercy to get her back into a restless doze until the next outcry. As I began to wear down, I contracted a stomach bug. There was initially some concern that it might be cholera. Some parts of the city were quarantined. We saw trucks bringing in bodies of victims and delivering suffering patients to the city hospital for treatment. None of these scenes triggered any "Christmas feelings" that I could identify.

I still had hopes that at one point in time, I would feel familiar festivity return. I wasn't depressed; just grasping at illusive ghosts to make the season "feel right." We chose a day for the whole family to shop for gifts in the town center. Stores did not really decorate much for the season, though we did pass a street vendor who was selling aluminum Christmas trees, the ilk of which was seen in Peanuts' cartoon strip. The sparse, metal branches on a silvery pole were a humorous representation of my efforts to make our traditions live in this country. Still, these signs of Christmas Present gave us merry-making opportunities. It was a season to be jolly as we looked into some strange and creative purchases for each other. Fa-la-la-la-la, lah-lah-lah-lahhhh!

Christmas Day, I was up before dawn icing five sheet cakes for the refreshments after the church program. The car had to be loaded with the puppet stage, props, and other paraphernalia. All eight of us had to be dressed and in our right minds by 0700 hours. Jim and I set out our Christmas surprise for the kids: one box of Kellogg's Rice Krispies, and one box of Corn Flakes. Though these did not fit regularly into our budget, it was worth the investment when we saw their eyes light up. Enthusiasm turned to polite quietness, once they began chewing. The flakes were stale and cardboard flavored. I checked the expiration date. Oh yeah! Two years old! We gave them permission to stop chewing. The family van was leaving, anyway, for the Kabalonga Boys' School, where Steve had booked the auditorium for all three churches to congregate.

I'll let Anne share from a letter she wrote to a family friend:

Christmas was pretty comical…The morning began at a way-too-early hour. We had to be out of the door at 7:30, so we sort of skipped sleeping in late or having an exquisite breakfast. I spent the trip to the building pulling curlers out of my hair, straightening my dress, frantically looking for something to pull my hair back with, and trying to keep a hyper-Mary under control.

*Once we arrived and got the stage and keyboard set up, and began the program with a puppet skit. Then we went to try to organize the refreshments. We made Kool-aid, shooed flies away, cut cakes, poured drinks, shooed flies away, covered cakes, shooed flies away, split napkins so there would be enough, shooed flies away, re-covered cakes, shooed flies away… you get the picture. When the whole program ended, we were **supposed** to hand out cake to the single-file lines parading past the table. (This was only a figment of an American's imagination.) Let me tell you, there were **NO SINGLE FILE LINES!!** We were mobbed at the table, and couldn't dish out cake fast enough…*

Let me fill in a bit. While the missionary kids were preparing refreshments for five hundred guests, I was inside directing the puppet program and accompanying the carols on our electric keyboard. Steve preached a short message and gave an invitation. Instructions for serving and receiving refreshments were given at the conclusion. The word "cake" must have triggered a response similar to the word "gold" in the West. There was absolutely nothing in their mindset that included waiting, standing in lines, or the idea of ONE piece. No sooner had the first ones received their cake, but many of them eased back into the lines for seconds, or tried to steal pieces off the tables. The missionary wives appealed to the guys to "patrol" the situation, give directions, and direct the traffic, but it was like trying to organize a stampede.

Back to Anne:

There were some guys trying to get control of things and figure out who had already had cake and who hadn't. We just laughed as Uncle Larry told all the kids to stick out their tongues so he could check for cake crumbs. Those kids were so greedy! It was ironic that the program they had just heard was about giving *and* not getting.

Seeing that the situation was hopelessly out of control, Larry ran to the van and pulled it up to the tables, telling the women and MKs to start putting the cake pans into the van. Sensing that it was a standoff of interests, the women from one church began grabbing the remaining pieces and tucking them into their bosoms for safekeeping and later distribution to their children. By this time, our eyeballs were standing on their stems. The missionary women had lost any sense of Christmas cheer, and the Africans seemed to have something between disgust and wonder at the reaction of "the greedy missionaries." The spirit of the program seemed smothered by this killer Phantom of Christmas Present.

Back to Anne's letter:

After we got home, no one was hungry, so we loafed around and played Rook with Dad while Mom and the younger kids slept. There had been no time to prepare food, so grazing took over. My entire consumption of my "Christmas feast" amounted to a couple pieces of cake, a few leftover crackers, and a couple bites of popcorn.

When we opened presents, there were so many smiles and surprises. My grandma sent us all mini-albums of our last few weeks with our cousins. I just sat on the floor and bawled. I miss them.

It was at the gift opening, that I had hoped the Christmas spirit would at last settle over us. Our family and friends had so richly blessed us with remembrances and sweet love, that we should have felt "visited." Instead, there was the stark reality of their absence from us. Both Jim and I said cheerful things about the gifts; but when Anne lost it, we all lost it. We sat on the floor midst Christmas paper and gifts and cried. The disconnect from family, the bizarre day, the culmination of longings for home and lusting for the familiar feelings of bygone days all converged into one flood of emotions. Even Rebecca joined in the spirit when she saw Mommy's sad countenance.

Jim, who was NOT crying, took over, "Ok. That's it. We are calling home!"

I looked at him pathetically, wincing at the thought of the cost. He knew what I was thinking, as we read one another's minds. "And I don't care what it costs," he emphasized.

Even I, the skinflint of the family, felt relief. All the presents and man made efforts at trying to recreate Christmas Past simply didn't cut it. We needed to hear our family's voices, to be together. I prayed that the telephone would work. What a God we have! He was touched with the feelings of our weaknesses! The call went through (this was an act of God!) to the family gathering at my sister Linda's home. We were all put on speaker phone there, and on our end everyone got their turn to hold the receiver. I don't know what it cost to this day, but whatever it was, it was worth it. When we hung up, satisfaction and peace marked our faces. Gifts, conversations, and enjoyment came as close to "normal" as I'd felt so far.

I went to bed all mixed up—happy because we'd connected with home, disappointed because Christmas had not been what I'd hoped. Maybe it was not supposed to be. It was supposed to be a joyful, celebrating day because Christ left home for us; because we had a Savior *with us*; because we were loved and given the perfect gift of eternal life! Instead, it had been a comedy of errors and felt like a failure in slow motion. I'd wanted to be close to Jesus on this day.

But then again, I remember thinking in a new way about Jesus Christ—what He must have felt as He left the comfort of His own Father's house for a life of poverty. On His "first Christmas" He was lying in a feedbox, bawling for milk. Knowing His sovereign rights and privileges, He chose to live with limitations in this foreign neighborhood of earth. I wondered if *He* compared *His* memories of paradise to this new place of hardships. I had a fresh respect for Jesus this year, for His humility to become one of us, to live among *us—as is*. Maybe this was the Spirit of Christmas Present. Maybe.

I fell into a tired sleep, wondering how long it takes to feel at home, to feel like you belong, to stop missing family and the States so much. All I knew was that I did not want to repeat this day, and I appreciated

Jesus' making the transition from heaven to earth—for us. His willingness, driven by love, was the Spirit of Christmas. Maybe one day, the Zambians would understand Christ's transition better because of ours. Maybe one day, I would forget myself and just live because of love—Christ's love. ***This was the Spirit of Christmas Past, Present, and Future.***

* * *

"The Word became flesh and dwelt among us..."[1]

In 1992
By Micah Chambers

The beginning of the year,
Was not a toast to cheer.
It started out so strange,
Its pattern never did change.

To start the year—this event was first,
My cousins' house into flames did burst.
Even though this sounds so weird,
My smooth faced uncle grew a beard.

That was just the start of ninety-two.
A baby sister changed my view.
Folding diapers became a habit.
When excitement came, I had to grab it.

Zambia, Africa became our next lot.
My first plane ride was not what I'd thought.
We lived in a home with twenty-one people,
While building a church without any steeple.

To raise the level of my cheer,
I found some friends that were actually near.
Ryan, Janine, and Harrison played
So I was glad that I had stayed.

Later that year a video came,
Barcelona's Olympics was the name.
Swimming, track, and gymnastics had a dream,
And Shannon Miller fulfilled it on the beam.

Now I've told you '92's plot.
If you didn't notice, it's quite a thought.
The year held its blacks and blues,
But that's the life God for me did choose.

Chapter 15

Coming Up for Air

This "becoming process" had a way of taking a toll on everyone. We needed time away. One of the beauties of a team is friendship. Larry and Sallie were true friends. They saw our need to regroup and offered to take the children so that we could have a couple nights at a motel. I came back only to nurse Rebecca, and then retreated to solitude at the hotel. I'd hoped the get-away would be "romantic," but Jim and I spent most of the time sawing logs in each other's face. Exhaustion took over intentions.

We returned to the Fogle's home refreshed. Not only had we rested, but our hopes were up. We'd spotted a rental in the classified ads of the Lusaka Times. It was in our price range, and near the church where we wanted to minister most. As soon as we returned, Jim made an appointment to see it. We needed to be out of the Southern Baptist housing by the end of January, so this was a break-through.

Meanwhile, the children needed a break from routines as much as we did. They'd been real troupers in school, amid the challenges of transplantation into foreign soil. We planned our first family vacation to Kafue, a small town about an hour from Lusaka, known for its wood carvings. The spirit of adventure settled over everyone. I packed survival supplies: cans of tuna, popcorn, carrots, etc., as well as the five-gallon Gott thermos of purified water.

The mountains just outside the city were a striking contrast to the concrete jungle and noise of the city. The main road south of Lusaka was mostly dirt with potholes made muddy by the rains. We jiggled our way towards Kafue, intrigued by the huts, the Africans walking alongside the road, the oxen and plows in the fields. After about forty-five minutes, we saw a sign announcing that we had arrived at Kafue. I'd expected to see shops and booths and signs to direct tourists to the wares of the carvers…or something. It was just a quiet little town, barely moving, very full of unhurried life. The wood carvers' shops were simple booths of crude, stick poles and plastic or mealie-meal bags.

Since the artwork was the reason we had come, we stopped to browse. We were the sole customers, it appeared, and there was clearly no other diversion for either us or the sellers anywhere in the town. That sparked some lively bartering and badgering, but did little to entertain the younger ones, who were poking at carved animals and playing in the dirt and rocks. I quickly discerned that Kafue was not the entertainment center of Africa; in fact, it was another adjustment—like Christmas—in our expectations. We would have to make special times *feel special* by developing our sense of adventure—without events or amusements, or bells and whistles. OK! We were up for it.

Back in the car, we drove toward Kafue River and the Rimo River Lodge. It was touted that one could go down in the evening and watch the hippos bathe and play. We rented a "chalet," which amounted to a cement cabin with metal, twin beds and cots, all in one room. There wasn't much to unpack, but we situated our water jug and baggage, and then looked at each other like, "now what?" There appeared to be no other guests in the cabins, nor was there indication of other activities to entertain clientele. We encouraged the kids to go exploring together before supper, warning them to watch for snakes and to stay back from the banks where there might be crocs. They headed down a path for the river, eager to see some hippos while Rebecca and I cat-napped.

Jim, and Rebecca, and I eventually sauntered down to the river bank. The children were skipping rocks and exploring their new territory. The scenery was exceptionally beautiful, unspoiled by any commercialism or ostentatious edifice. The broad river was blue as the sky, with a backdrop of mountains and undeveloped woodlands. A Zambian fisherman in a dugout canoe glided across the water, spreading his fishing net. It was the only movement to attract attention. We shushed Rebecca and Mary, and lowered our voices to a whisper in hopes of encouraging the hippos to surface. For over an hour we strained our eyes and craned our necks for the slightest splash. Just in case the grey masses in the middle of the river were hippos, we took pictures. Ironically, they must have posed for a very long time because those "hippos" never moved a muscle. At sunset, we headed for the chalet, having stocked up on fresh air and hopes.

In the absence of amusements or activities, we decided to get dressed up for supper, make an "event" of the evening meal. All eight of us slicked up and walked together to the restaurant. It was closed. The only building with signs of life was a bar-restaurant pavilion, a semi-enclosed, thatch-and-pole structure. Country western music blared from the speakers for three women and a man with slurry speech. Upon entering the shelter, we seated ourselves around two small tables. Neither of the two waitresses appeared interested in us or in any business—other than for the man with the beer.

We waited ten minutes to be "noticed" in the otherwise empty room. The women seemed falsely absorbed in a conversation, while casting glances at this white spectacle of a family of eight. Finally, Jim signaled to the woman plump enough to be the cook. She shuffled over, appearing indifferent to the situation, but probably just intimidated by the foreigners. Jim asked, "Could we please have a menu?"

The woman looked a bit annoyed, but padded off silently to find a menu. She returned about ten minutes later with ONE "menu," a hand-printed piece of cardboard box with about ten items and two options for drinks. "We have chicken and mutton curry," she muttered, as she stood there, ink pen in hand.

Jim thanked her and asked for a few minutes to decide. We all wondered what that curry announcement was for. No one was interested in curry of any kind, having had it the previous night, so we collaborated over the choices. After about five minutes, he again signaled that we were ready to order, and she ambled back to our tables.

"We'd like seven Rimo burgers with chips," Jim enunciated carefully.

"I SAID we have chicken and mutton curry!" Her tone hinted annoyance that we had not registered her comment about the curry.

"Oh! You mean that is ALL the choices?" She raised her eyebrows. By this time we read body language better. "And we have two portions of Rimo burgers," she added.

OK. We hiked up the decibels to place our order over the music system: two portions of Rimo burger with "chips" (French fries), two mutton curries with rice, and three chicken curries. For drinks, we wanted four Cokes and two orange Fantas. The waitress returned in her flat, unenthused manner, telling us that there were no Cokes. She said we could have orange Fanta or water. We adjusted again, asking if the water was boiled. Again, the questions noticeably irritated the woman. No, the water was not boiled. She acted as if we had insulted them, but all we wanted to know was if it was safe. OK. That would be six orange Fantas then. The waitress wrote her order on a brown cardboard box flap.

Thirty minutes and one side of the country western tape later, we were served two exceedingly dry Rimo burgers with a side portion of fried cabbage over rice. Nathan and I dug into our mutton curry, and spent the remainder of the time having a contest over who had the biggest pile of bone splinters. I think I won, with thirty-some. I imagined them butchering this poor sheep with a chain saw, though it was not a very kind thought. The chicken curry was quite good, so we all sampled the other's leftovers. We were still hungry, but it appeared that we had cleaned out the kitchen and intruded into the routines of the management long enough.

With the evening event drawing to a close, we paid our bill, thanked the relieved waitress, and made our way back down the dark path to the chalet. There was laughter in the night as we reviewed our big event for the day—supper with a country twang. Back at the cabin, we were all longing for something a little more satisfying, so we rummaged through our bags for snacks and desserts. The novelty of eating African and sleeping on cots was enough to classify this as another family adventure. We lay under mosquito nets and listened to the night sounds until we fell asleep.

The next two days, we avoided the restaurant and ate tuna fish or peanut butter sandwiches. With no agenda, and no events, and no hippos to be seen, we hiked and explored the area leisurely, loving creation and each other's attention. The fresh air and scenery invigorated us. When we were alone in the chalet, we played family games, read books, and slept off weariness. Our grand finale was the last day of 1992: we drove up the mountain road to overlook the magnificent expanse of Kafue Gorge. The undeveloped forest was dotted with occasional huts and wisps of cooking fires, but nothing appeared to disturb its natural beauty, not even the main road which snaked its way through the trees. The broad Kafue River twisted lazily into the valley and out again, making its way towards the city, as we would soon do.

Before leaving, we took time to gaze over miles and miles of vast, unhurried valley life.

The rural culture was quite different from the city life and scenes we had experienced thus far. The exposure was enough to plant seeds of curiosity and wonderment whether we would ever live outside the borders of our concrete jungle. For us, for now, we were becoming city dwellers, and that was as big a leap for us culturally as this gorge. Right then, our food was gone and our water supplies low. That was our clue to head back home. In the town of Kafue, we stopped at the woodcarvers to barter for some gifts and a huge, carved rhino that Nathan wanted.

Jiggling back over the muddy road to Lusaka, I felt happy. There wasn't much to do; not much to say that we did, but everyone had been together, away, and satisfied by our explorations. No one was grumbling. We seemed to need a lot of nothing-to-do, a lot of fresh air, a lot of one another, without interruptions. Our family was fun, its own amusement. God knew what the next weeks would hold, and these few days of solitude were sandwiched in between the thick slices of life—the bottom of 1992 and the top of 1993. I wrote as soon as I returned home, "It feels good to feel good."

* * *

"He restores my soul."[1]

Chapter 16

And Here Is Your Change

The change of the calendar year kicked off a series of other changes. The very next day, January 2nd, Mary's age changed. According to her, she was changing from two to "three-teen." She had an opinion for anyone who might ask, and for those who didn't, it was her opinion that they SHOULD ask—HER, of course.

A birthday package arrived from the States in a brown manila envelope. Among other things, a supporting church had sent some Mickey Mouse tissues in a purse-size packet. Mary—as usual—dove right into these novelties, demonstrating how the tissue "worked." When she was finished blowing and wiping, she announced her satisfaction with the product, "Hmmmph! It matches my nose!" Mary was our Anne of Green Gables; she never lacked for words, nor we for laughter, no matter the occasion.

With the beginning of a new year, I was in hopes of beginning a new change of pace. Our ministry was so broad, it lacked centrality and encouraged "hecticity." When our feet waded into an ocean of ministry, we nearly drowned in waves of compassion and adjustment. Now, we just wanted to learn to swim in this ocean—settle into a constructive use of energy, rather than expending so much time running from beach to beach. Jim's experience before Christmas of filling Steve's role as church planter had given him an appetite to lead one of these flocks. We'd begun to pray about a change in the way we did ministry. God seemed to be awakening in him a desire to pastor the congregation at Chilenji. We put it before the team for their input.

Yet another change was upon us, whether we liked it or not. We had to change houses within the next six weeks. Our contract with the Southern Baptists was about up. As soon as vacation ended, we headed for the phone to set up a time to see the house that we'd seen listed in the paper. When Jim called, the guy answered with, "We're only looking for executive-type people for this place."

Jim responded with, "Oh, we probably won't fit that description; we're missionaries. And…we probably can't afford it." The man's response encouraged us to look at it anyway, so we set an appointment. We were getting desperate to find something within our unrealistic budget. Other small places were going for $1000-$1500, and we had a whole $500/month to work with. The lure of extra space for our family of eight was a real draw, but even better, this house was actually only a mile from Chilenji, the church Jim wanted to assist. Our hopes were high and our prayers intense as we headed to Woodlands Extension to see this place.

The house was a has-been mansion: six bedrooms, four bathrooms, huge kitchen, office, dining and living room, walk-in pantry, laundry room, interior courtyard, two-car carport, and self-contained guest room. At one time in its glory days, it had served the German Embassy as a guest accommodation. The key was that it was in quite a state of disrepair and filth. That made it negotiable. Jim made our crazy $500 bid on it and was accepted! We looked to God with wonder; how does He do that? Answer: "Before they call, I will answer, and while they are yet speaking, I will hear."[1]

We set to work immediately. Naturally, we had more than a few changes to make. The pink exterior with black, shiny trim "wasn't Rachel." Neither were the cockroaches, odors, broken doors and windows, neglected yard, and plumbing disasters. We hired an exterminator for the roaches, ants, ticks and other insects, but no one warned us about the rats that had accumulated, feeding on the raw heaps of garbage in the yard and house. We hired some guys to dig a new garbage pit for starters. Two painters were hired for the interior, and the entire missionary team spent a day replacing broken windows, cleaning, and repairing. Some of the missionaries said they never would have tackled the property, but they were sweetly willing to help us anyway.

The change of pace we'd hoped for occurred, but not for the better. Just as we began working on the new house, the building plans for the church building at Chawama were cleared by the government. The rush was on for Jim to construct a pavilion-like shelter—stage one of the church building. While it was a simple structure, the timing could not have been more challenging to Jim or to me. Meanwhile, the weekend ministry with youth continued, as well as a new course we were developing and teaching at the Bible Institute: Marriage and the Christian Family. Besides the eleven children at the house and the ministry responsibilities, all the packing for the move fell to my over-sight. Jim worked most days at the church or at the new house, or under the van, trying to keep life in its engine. The VW Combie was becoming a continual threat to our sanity and safety. By now it was guzzling five quarts of oil per week, and worse yet, it was not quiet about its unreasonable demands on us. It backfired like a regular Tin Lizzy from Appalachia, every twenty or thirty seconds. Riding in it was nothing less than an embarrassing invitation to stress.

It was only two weeks from our sweet little vacation getaway, and we were already feeling ragged. On January 16th, Rebecca woke up crying. She had severe diarrhea and cramping every fifteen to twenty minutes. By 10:00 that morning, her stools had become bloody. Though I was nursing her, she was dehydrating very quickly. I could do nothing more than plead with God to send Jim home. He was in town looking for car parts for the sick van, completely unaware of our trauma. We had no way to communicate to him what was happening, so I cried out desperately to God.

After about an hour, I heard the sweet backfiring of our Tin Lizzy at the gate. As soon as Jim assessed the situation, we headed back through the gate with Rebecca draped over my shoulder—limp as a little rag doll. The black smoke had barely cleared before we re-polluted the air in the rush to get to one of the European-run clinics. Bang! Pop-pop!

A red-headed, female doctor took Rebecca's limp form from my arms. Seeing the baby's dehydration, she immediately started an IV of fluids and began chewing me out for waiting so long to bring her in. It had been four hours from the time she first started the diarrhea. I explained I had no car, and her brash mannerisms softened a little. I was hurt and scared over Rebecca; frustrated and worn from too much stress and too much of Tin Lizzy.

The lab tests showed amoebic dysentery. After the drip was complete and antibiotics were started, we were released. Though the trauma was undesirable, it brought into perspective what was really important in all this white-water living. The next day, I wrote my parents, "I'm so happy that the Lord is only a prayer away... It's such a precious blessing to hear Becca laughing and even crying without pain!" Jim added, "The engine problem seemed to pale when we considered the possibility of one of our children losing strength and possibly even life."

I'd hoped the pressure might let up. It didn't. With deadlines coming up, we had to postpone moving for one week so that Jim could finish the church roof. Then we received word that two couples were coming to the field to visit: one was the field administrator for the mission and the other, a board member from our home church, Ken and Ida St. Clair. I wanted to show off the new house. I scrubbed and disinfected everything for the move, but the guards and painters left their food all over, inviting in more roaches and ants. We fumigated and were frustrated all over again!

God's promises became very personal to me. I wrote in my journal a paraphrase of 1 Corinthians 10:13: *The temptation to anxiety is taking over you. It's a common one. But, God is faithful. He will not let you go over the edge, but will in the midst of this temptation, make a way of escape, that you may be able to bear it.* Prayer was an escape I used, and—frankly—so was humor.

One morning I woke up about dawn and walked to the bathroom to assess the night's toll in the mirror. "Very weathered," I pronounced myself. In my peripheral vision, I saw something long and brown hanging out of the bathtub overflow drain. At first I thought it was a glob of Anne's hair, but getting a closer look, I realized it was a tail, about five inches of ugly. My fear of snakes, particularly in the house, made me suck in air and head for Jim, still asleep in the room.

"Honey?" I crooned, steadying my voice to a breathy level. "There's something I need you to take care of in the bathroom." I was trying to announce this calmly, enticingly, as if offering coffee and donuts.

"What," he grunted, half present on the pillow.

"Well, someone's tail is sticking out of the drainpipe in the tub, and I don't want to know whose it is."

My hero lumbered out of bed and into the bathroom. When he could focus, he assessed that it was not a snake but a lizard. Being the man that he was, he chose his weapon, Rebecca's nose aspirator, and squeezed air onto the visitor's tail. It removed its unsightly backside from sight. My toes uncurled in my sandals. God seemed to chase anxiety with some of the off-the-wall stuff. It made days bearable. Then, Mary's off-the-wall spontaneity made things downright funny. Later, I heard her singing at the top of her lungs, "We're OFF! to see the lizard, the wunnerful lizard of all." If nothing else was growing, our sense of humor was.

One morning, Jim had to work at the new house, and it fell to my lot to drive the children to school across the city, about twenty minutes from our home. I hated driving in the morning rush-hour anyway, but sitting in traffic with a car which exploded out the tailpipe every few seconds was like volunteering to become a spectacle. I had no choice. The children had to get to school, and I was the designated driver. We piled into the car and took off, the Beverly Hillbillies in living color, backfiring multiple times before the yard boy opened the gate. No one had trouble tracing us: we were spewing black clouds of oil all the way down the street. I was trying to console myself that this must be the cross of a missionary—humiliation—and I must bear it bravely. I felt like crawling under a rock.

Once we were on Great East Road, I accelerated, hoping that speed would help these engine hiccups and reduce the black and cloudy pillar in our wake. It did! However, there were speed limits as well as traffic lights. I sighed and slowed down. The stoplight was just turning red.

We were soon surrounded, backfiring loudly and puffing smoky exhaust behind us. I tried staring ahead, looking dignified, as if we were not a spectacle; but the hypocrisy felt worse than the reality. The embarrassment and self-consciousness was contagious within the car. The kids made comments: "I wish we didn't have to drive this. It is so embarrassing! Everybody is looking at us!" Nathan, his usual, optimistic self, consoled everybody with something like "Let's make the most of it!"

"Smile at them when they stare," I challenged them. I tried it myself with the driver in a white car next to us. However, I could not hold his gaze for long. I quickly diverted my attention to adjusting the rear view mirror and checking out the dashboard instruments. Bang! Pop! We were collecting more attention, and I could feel the blood creeping up my neck. Pop-pop! BANG! The red light resisted green. What was wrong with the stupid timer on that light?!

"We certainly cannot pretend our way out of this one, kids." I turned to the man in the car next to us and over enunciated, "Don't mind us: we're just passing gas!" The kids just split up. The light turned green, and I stepped on the gas, only to shower the car behind us with black smoke. "Sorry, everybody!" I apologized into the air.

Obviously, it was time for a change of vehicles. We had neither money nor options, but God—who always causes us to triumph—has ways of providing manna in the wilderness and oil in empty clay pots. I had no idea how, but somehow, God would do something. He had to.

Meanwhile, we limped along, praying for life extensions for the VW. I wrote: "I'm chugging in first gear. I've had very little sleep this week, as we are in between houses. Delays, uncertainties, undependable promises, and the African culture in general have been stretching me, along with the changes. Seems right now like all our afflictions are coming in bunches—Rebecca's dysentery, the dead van, a prolonged move, living in disarray, boxes and bare walls—I'm really feeling fragile. Would appreciate prayer," I sent that out as an SOS.

The van lasted two more weeks after the move. Oil addiction took it. It coughed its last, smoky breath after sputtering and backfiring rebelliously into the new yard. We laid it to rest, and a new engine was the only hope for resurrection. But, until then, Steve loaned us his six-ton Mercedes Benz truck, unmistakably watermelon-green and big as a whale. Zambians and Chambers spilled out of it each Sunday morning

Jim operates on Tin Lizzy

102

like little black and white seeds. Life was an adventure, if you kept perspective, and that was the key: keeping perspective.

By this time, the team had approved our new church focus: the Chilenji congregation. The change in ministry was a boost to our spirits. We felt like we were settling down to a spiritual home, a place to hang our hearts and efforts. God had placed us strategically close to this work, in an ex-pink mansion over the hilltop, with a remarkable vehicle for gathering children's attention. Our guests, the St. Clairs and Goughs, arrived one week after we moved in, and Mr. St. Clair—whose eye for a good car was in his heart—returned to our home church to raise funds for a new engine. Jim's home church also took up an offering to complete the funds needed.

A couple weeks later, short termer, Dan Harp, arrived on the field, helping with the change of the VW engine and other jobs. GOD WAS FAITHFUL in every change we faced, and patient in our anxious moments. I was supposed to know this in theory, but God wanted us to experience it in life, so we did. One of the Puritan writers testified, "I bless thee for tempering every distress with joy; too much of the former might weigh me down; too much of the latter might puff me up. Thou art wise to give me a taste of both."[2]

* * *

> *"Be still my soul: the Lord is on thy side;*
> *Bear patiently the cross of grief or pain:*
> *Leave to thy God to order and provide;*
> *In every change he faithful will remain.*
> *Be still my soul: thy best, thy heav'nly Friend*
> *Through thorny ways leads to a joyful end."*[3]

Chapter 17

When I Get Big

I suppose we all have an ideal in our minds of what we OUGHT to be like. It is ever before us as an image we strive to become, or else a consciousness of what we are not. That ideal is a subliminal yardstick for measuring ourselves, our progress, or our setbacks. For the Christian, the ideal should be the image of Christ, growing up to live and to think and to feel like He does, regardless of the context into which we are thrust. If I could just keep my eyes on that Image! David said, "I have set the Lord always before me."[1] Paul even described how this is done. "We...beholding as in a *mirror the glory of the Lord, are being transformed into the same image* from glory to glory..."[2]

Being thrust into missions, where everything around us changed, had a way of exaggerating everything in us which was NOT like Christ. I wanted more desperately to grow into that image, to be *like* Christ in every context, but I looked like such a pygmy compared to Him. Nevertheless, our shortcomings were cause for us to back up against the wall and be measured next to His tall image—again, and again, and again. It caused us to step back from "our mark on the wall" and take another long look at Him, at His full stature. Looking at His image in this different context made me more in awe of His full height than ever before.

One night at the supper table, Mary announced with conviction, "When I get big, I'm gonna grow up!" There was laughter at her random logic, but a thought took root. As obvious as it sounds, getting big spiritually and reaching closer to the measure of Christ would take some growing up on our part. It would take more than desire to be big; it would take more than imagining we *are* big; it would take more than praying to become big. Getting big would come through: big experiences, tests (if you will), hard times, and uncomfortable circumstances. These would make us lean on God and not on ourselves, and *that* would be "growing up."

The following letters describe some growth pains and growth spurts that came in the next months. These experiences made us sense our weakness, our shortness—rather than boosting a big image of our own capabilities. Feeling weak, we ran to the Bread of Life, the Word, hungry for strength beyond ourselves. We ate, and we lived. Then, we grew a little at a time. Missionaries, no matter how old when they hit the field, still have to grow one challenge at a time. The image of Christ is always bigger than they.

The recipients of these letters were people we trusted, our support team of family and believing friends. How would we have developed without them listening, caring, praying, encouraging, and enabling us to press on? I do not know, and I thank God we never had to find out!

Excerpts from Jim's letter, March 29, 1993:

It runs! It really does! The van engine has been replaced and amazingly, it runs and doesn't backfire or use a gallon or more of oil a week. Praise the Lord for His loving-kindness! And praise Him for those who gave of their own finances to enable us to get the new engine parts. It was a real blessing to see the way that the Lord used so many of you to be a help to us. We praise God for you, each one. We know, too, that many of you prayed diligently for us during this time, and we could not have made it through without those prayers. [He then proceeds with a man-sized explanation of what he went through to get the new engine installed, fine tuned, one various engine part and dysfunction at a time.] This was a real trial for me. Thank you again—each one—for your prayers.

I have had other trials of late, too. I was following a funeral

105

procession in the Mercedes Benz truck. I was on my way with the MKs (missionary kids) to one of our weekly meetings. I had one person left to pick up, and we were slowly proceeding in a line of about fifteen vehicles. As I approached the turn-off, I turned on my turn-signal for the entrance of the school. I barely got halfway across the other side of the road, when a smaller Toyota pickup really surprised me. He was going so fast that he did not have time to hit his brakes or blow his horn. Witnesses said later that he had tried to pass at least ten cars before he hit me. The driver then had the gall to blame me for not seeing him in my rear view mirror or waiting until he passed me! Needless to say, this did not make me happy. Get this; he has just hit a big six-ton truck, practically ripping the bumper off and tearing his passenger door nearly off, and he says that he only had one car between us when he pulled out. When the police woman asked him how he could do that kind of damage in such a short distance, he explained that his truck engine is "VERY POWERFUL AND ACCELERATES VERY FAST." It was very hard not to laugh out loud. As I went to the police station, there were two plain clothes detectives there who "just happened" to be at the accident scene. They explained fully that I was completely in the right, and that the man had tried to pass at least ten cars before hitting me. I was grateful to see how God was protecting me from possible injustice. After dealing with this engine mess, I do not think that I can take much more.

As I got home from the accident, I found Rachel ready to take Rebecca down the street to the clinic. She had been running a low-grade fever off and on for five days. We found that she has a yeast infection [Result of dysentery meds] that will have to be treated for three weeks. Now, ten days later she still has not responded to the treatment. Her fever will go up and down. At times we think she is coming out of it, and then back comes the fever. WE trust God that He will bring her safely through.

My main purpose in writing, though, is not to load you folks down with all our troubles. We just want to give praise to God for all that He has graciously done. When we are weak, then He is able to show His strength.

The new church work is progressing slowly. The afternoon service on Sundays is held in our carport. We have a couple of people come who we know are not presently believers, two cousins Aggree and Alex. It is a joy to hear them say that they have never had anyone involve them in the study of God's Word personally...I know they are interested, but I do not know how much. Aggree is also trying to help me get a telephone.

At the same time, the adults are meeting on Sunday afternoon, Sherry Segal is teaching a class for the youth—basics of Bible knowledge. The class culminates in a volleyball activity or game, led by Nathan. It is neat to see the Lord use each of the kids in some way or another.

A letter of my own describes what I was observing of family growth pains, too:

Please pray for Nathan. Relationship choices are limited. His special friend has become infatuated with a guy who is a real "flash-in-the-pan" sort—genuinely artificial. She is keeping him "at bay," so he is hurting. He's also struggling with two courses—Advanced Biology and Auto Mechanics. The instructor for the Auto Mechanics class is a MECHANIC, not a teacher. His tests are not evaluations of real knowledge. [The blank is connected to the blank. Yeah, right!] Nathan is discouraged; so are we, but he gets what he can and is eager to apply what he knows. Glad he is an optimist!

Another unspoken reality is that Nathan is facing his sixteenth birthday in a few weeks. All his friends are getting their driving licenses, a real mile-marker for manhood. He cannot. Legal driving age for Zambia is eighteen.

Anne is noticeably lonely. Pray about us finding other decent friends that are NOT MKs. Aimee and Darla are still her good friends, but others would be appreciated too. She sure is aware of boys—but is not acting stupid around them—all part of growing up.

Meg is into puberty, and has all the symptoms. She always was emotional, but now she is… well… EMOTIONAL!!!! She seems to collect friends wherever she goes. Friends are her "ministry."

Micah needs more friends. Ryan Fogle and he have a couple things in common; they both love messes and Legos and dislike school work. However, a little variety would be good for both of them. Meg and Harrison are so close, they often leave him out. Mary is a good playmate for him, especially since she is three, going on fourteen. However, her friends are secondary to "Mom and family." She's doing great. One of the benefits of a large family is that we have one another for companionship. WE can, however, get in-grown.

Jim and I are reaching for the surface after being under for the third time. WE have made an appointment with each other for Friday afternoon. The strain of ministry is HEAVY. I need to get my footing after the move. My soul has been tried, and yet the Shepherd keeps restoring it. It's a good thing. I've been too close to serious depression—so many emotional and physical demands all in a few months.

Anne writes:

My closest friends have been my books lately… Darla Bell has made life more bearable than I'd allowed myself to hope. She's an athletic, down-to-earth girl with a schedule like mine—pressured with school and helping busy mothers out of the bothers of cooking and cleaning. She's been really nice, but lately, she's had her head in the clouds. She's really taken to a guy, but he has a way of flirting with the girls he likes and making everyone else feel as privileged as dog biscuits. So, while she's preoccupied with him, I've resorted to something more consistent than guys: books!

And that's another thing, I was feeling sorry for myself the other day. I am realizing that I'll be at least sixteen before I have my first boyfriend. With my parents' protection and my looks, probably eighteen! Oh well, I'm really growing in the Lord a lot!?

Another letter from me on March 15, 1993

Hey you guys,

It is really late, and my splitting headache tells me I'd better keep it short. President Chiluba has called for a state of emergency, due to a plan by the former government (UNIP) to reinstate their party. That means we are to carry our IDs everywhere and abide by a curfew. Anyone out after 8 p.m. can be arrested. I hope we don't have any evening emergencies, especially with no phone. So far, there is nothing alarming to be seen in the streets except for military police and various law enforcement squads in increasing numbers…

What else is news? Well, we have had over one week of an overflowing sewer in our yard. Pee-yew! Jim is getting to know the city council guys real well. They take everything so leisurely, and wonder why cholera is a problem! The city had just recovered from a cholera outbreak a month before. Well, time to get our minds out of the sewer.

We are still battling three-inch cockroaches, and our Zambian paint job over the pink exterior is washing off with the rains. Hmmm. Do you guys get the idea that I ought to stop this letter for tonight and finish when my perspective is a bit brighter? I think so! The only stuff I can think of at this hour is Puddleglum-type information. I'll try again in the morning, when the brain and body are sweeter. Hopefully…

Oh yeah! I thought of one really happy tidbit. Jim turned forty, and I threw a surprise party… there was plenty of good food. Jim had requested I make his birthday cake as a replica of our house in Cedarville. I did, and I put all forty candles in the roof of the house. It was a true house afire. The day had memories of laughter in it; the team has fun together.

I have been reading a good book Tom and Bev sent us. It's been the encouragement I've needed when searching for stability, normalcy, and a routine... there are just too many changes going on. Probably the one that fazes me the most is the changes in Jim. I see his interests, attention, approaches, and even his capabilities changing right in front of my eyes. I'm referring to his drive to pastor this work, his initiative to lead us, his desire to prepare sermons. It's been a little bit shocking to me, since I've lived with a guy who usually put his efforts into pipes, hammers, drywall plaster, and so forth. It seems like God is changing the course of our lives, and though I've waited seventeen plus years for some of these changes, I almost don't feel ready for them. So pray I'll learn to find joy in all the change. It's about blowing me away.

After feeling so stretched and pulled by the unrelenting adjustments, we were supposed to be growing into the stature of Christ. I wanted that. I just did not anticipate the process of growing up. In the kindness of God, the St. Clairs brought out several love gifts and bolstering messages from family and friends. One of these was a videotape of my sister singing "He Loved Me," a song from Romans 8. I wrote this response:

Lin, don't know what time it is. I got up at 4:30—as usual—facing a little reluctantly the day. I'm tired, and I'm tired of irritations— which seem out of proportion when I AM TIRED! So, I read my Bible, prayed, and turned on the video you guys sent out. One line of your song began "He chose me..." I never sit through that without crying and this morning was no exception, but as my heart was listening my mind was rewording—no, interpreting—it to my situation:

"What shall separate me from the love of God? Shall mosquitoes or the five-day, backed up sewer? Shall sleeplessness or endless days of rain, a weary soul or children with worms? Or one thousand cockroaches? Or the threat of cholera? No, I am persuaded (but forgetful) that none of these things shall separate me from the love of God which is in Christ Jesus."

I sure miss you, especially when I see you singing. I just imagined you hugging me, and it felt good. I know you would if you could. I've thought of you, appreciated you, needed you, prayed for you, and loved you with all my thoughts and feelings. Try to send me a note just to let me see your personal handwriting. It matters. I love you so much.

I wasn't sure why frustrations came all at once, as if we should not catch our breath or our composure. The unpredictable (truck accident, plugged sewers, government state of emergency) merged with uncertainty (Rebecca's fevers, ministry adjustments, pending phone without service, lonely kids) and unpleasant facts of life (changing a car engine, worms in the children, roaches in cupboards, rats in the attic). All these things left our mouths agape. Some days, I wonder if I even thought about how Jesus would live this out. I just lived through it, feeling short in stature as a Christian and very tired. Nevertheless, God made ways to bear it so that we could grow up. Connectedness to the family of Christ was how He did it with teammates, national believers, letters, calls, video tapes, and relationships from afar.

＊ ＊ ＊

"Looking unto Jesus…who for the JOY
that was set before Him endured…"[3]

Prayer Letter April 1993

To Churches and Supporters

Brrring… brrring… Hullo? You have reached the Chambers' residence. Although we are unable to answer the phone at this time, due to the absence of one, we ask you to continue leaving your names, phone numbers, and messages. WE will attempt to return your communiqué as soon as… as soon as… we ever catch up. Rachel just discovered a box from the move marked "miscellaneous." It contained UNMAILED thank-yous for Christmas gifts. Gulp! Please don't hang up. The connection is sometimes pretty poor, especially at this end, but rest assured, the reception at this end is clear. Sorry we keep cutting out.

If you've forgiven and desire further information on happenings in our hemisphere, please press #1.

#1 Life has been exhilarating and exhausting, perplexing and perpetual. The work visit from Dan Harp was exhilarating; so was the news that Cedarville College is sending a summer ministry team, led by our friends Byron and Libby Shearer. The anticipation is the exhausting part: isn't waiting hard?!

Meanwhile, other incidents have taken extra effort; Jim and the MKs were involved in an accident with the six-ton truck. God's faithfulness provided their protection. The other driver took full responsibility, since the Lord strategically positioned many eyewitnesses, including two plain-clothes policemen. The aftermath of paperwork and responsibilities is annoying but necessary.

Another "biggie" was Jim's money pouch being stolen from the truck seat. The thieves removed the money, returned all his important papers inside the pouch, and tossed the bag in the back of the truck. Again, God's intervention preserved Jim from long hours and long lines replacing documents. What a mighty God we serve!

A further factor exhausting us is Rebecca's health. She ran a cycle of unexplained fevers, vomiting, general discomfort, fitful sleep, and trips to the clinic. Today, a new clinic, an American doctor, and medicine for MALARIA encouraged us. She is sleeping quietly tonight. NO FEVER.

For further information on the ministry, press #2.

#2 You will remember we are in new territory as pastor of the Chilenje congregation. Although the youth/children's ministry is consistently running eighty to ninety, committed adults are few. One of our faithful men died suddenly April 3rd. Our family ministered to his unsaved friends and relatives the days prior to burial, seeing sights and hearing sounds we've never heard before. More on that later...

Other briefs on the ministry: We began a Sunday afternoon Bible study. Rachel holds a discipleship/sewing class for five girls recently saved. Anne and Megan teach fifty-plus children for Sunday School, while Nathan and Sherry Segal head up the teen class of thirty to forty regulars. While all of this is exciting, we continue to need special prayer for the adult ministry. We hear that we are gaining credibility, especially as Africans see spiritual consistency and care for one another. A church building is necessary to promote a sense of permanency. Please do not forget to pray for both, as well as for our personal lives. We get tired.

The team has invested in a recently discovered Nyanja coach… Please pray for our minds; we have an absorption rate of about .5%.

If interested in family news-bits, please press #3.

#3 Three Chambers had birthdays. As a result of the aging process one lost a few pearlies, now speaking with a listhp; one gained a few pounds and some silver locks; and one wants to see his picture on a driver's license. Guess who?

Despite the "Fascinating Facts" article sent to us by Roy Carr, we still hate the reappearing varmints. "Did you know a cockroach, if touched by human fingers, will wash itself vigorously, trying to get the human gunk off?" The feeling is mutual.

Mary: Mom, when are we going to get to Africa? (place of adventure)

Mom: Why Mary! You know where we are! Where are we?

Mary: (wrinkling up her nose) We are just HOME, mom.

Thank you for using AT&P (a telephone and postal) communications. We regret to inform you that your time is up. If you wish to continue, please lick a stamp. Goodbye! Hmmmm. Click.

— *The Chambers Family*

Chapter 18

Stung by Death

"Oh death, where is thy sting? Oh grave, where is thy victory?"[1]

The "Marriage and the Family" class at the Bible Institute was drawing to a close. Jim and I loved team teaching this class, especially since the Zambians considered it a hot topic of interest. Actually, we had very little firsthand knowledge about the real issues facing African marriages, but marital stress was common and normal. We dealt with these each week at the Lusaka Hotel conference room, one of our temporary buildings for the Institute.

One of our brightest students was a man from our Chilenje congregation, Jazzy White Banda. He was an inquisitive student in his thirties, unhappily married, but trying to learn in earnest what he could do to improve that relationship. Jazzy was one of the few students who dared ask questions in class. He asked because he intended to do something with the knowledge. He was a growing and hungry Christian! I loved that about him.

The last week of the term, Jazzy became ill and sent word with another student that he was too sick to come for the final exam. As class was finishing, the hotel desk clerk came upstairs to our room, saying there was a phone call for us. I was puzzled, as it had to be important or else very urgent to have us paged. I went to the phone.

A female with a Zambian accent greeted me with all the customary amenities. Once past these, she informed me that she was bringing a message from Mr. Jazzy Banda: he would be unable to come for his final examination, she said. I assured her that a student had conveyed this, and we understood; we would be praying for him to get well. I asked if this was his wife, and she said no. She was the nurse at UTH (University Teaching Hospital.) She reiterated that Mr. Banda was "very, very sick" and that it would be good if we could come to see him. I assured her that we could not come right now because of class, but that we would try to do that over the weekend. I asked her to give a message to Jazzy of our prayers, and that there was no problem about the examination; we would help him to make it up.

I felt like we had covered all the bases, so began to close down the conversation. I was very impressed with his conscientiousness over class responsibilities. We exchanged goodbyes, but I felt puzzled by the tone of the nurse. It sounded like Jazzy had come down with something rather serious; or was she just reflecting concern that we come to visit him? I didn't know. I wished I did. This indirect communication style was such a guessing game—and very frustrating!

Saturday was the usual blur of activity. We were preparing for our family vacation the next week, as well as all the preparations for Sunday—lesson preps, sermon notes, youth activities. By the time of the evening hospital visitation hours, we were tired and decided to visit Jazzy on Sunday afternoon. Maybe he would be discharged by then.

The next morning, we drove into Mr. Mutantika's yard where we usually met for church. As soon as we piled out of the van, the kids began unloading the easel, teaching board, straw mats, wooden stools, and other paraphernalia. After greeting a few adults, I struck up a conversation with Mr. Mutantika, the elderly gentleman who hosted our church at his house.

"Good morning Mr. Mutantika!" I said enthusiastically. "How are you?"

"Fine," came the standard and inevitable answer. But I did not expect the next, direct question. "Did you know that Jazzy was sick?"

"Yes! I found out Friday, when he called in sick for his final examination at Bible Institute. How is he now? Do you know? We're planning to visit him at the hospital this afternoon. Is he still admitted, or did he go home?"

"He is dead," was his soft-spoken reply.

I leaned forward, my eyes bugging out. "What? What did you say?"

"He passed away last night at UTH. His mother was with him, at his bedside."

I was staggering with this reality, taken completely off guard. The nurse's voice replayed in my mind. Why didn't she tell me he was dying! Why? Why didn't I catch on to the seriousness of his illness? Is that what she meant when she said, "very, very?" In America, we would have been up front. I had noticed he had been losing weight, but this was so sudden. He'd been at class a week before and at church last Sunday. As I continued mulling over this reality, Jim took charge of the conversation, getting details and directions from Mr. Mutantika about our involvement in the funeral. I went to a corner of Mutantika's yard to be by myself for a moment, to cry. A heavy spirit settled on me.

While I had been present at some funerals, I had not *participated* in one. As the new pastor's wife, I really did not know protocol or culture well enough to feel that my role could be appropriately fulfilled, at least to *their* satisfaction. As soon as church was dismissed, I went to Banda—our house help—to ask him what to do. It was important to do this right, I felt sick that we had not been there, and angry that we were so naïve about these things! The intensity of my feelings exploded like a freshly released fire hydrant. "Banda! What do I wear? What do I do? Tell me everything you can think of. We don't do funerals the same in America." It was imperative that he be meticulous with the details.

The next hour was a Q and A session between Banda and me. First, it was clothing: Banda said I would HAVE to wear a chitenge and a chitembala, a wrap-around cloth for women and a head covering, both signs of respect and appropriateness. I countered with questions to clarify why and how each thing was to be done. I could see that a shopping trip to Town Center was a necessity. Then we reviewed protocol: I would need to remove my shoes at the door of the house;

greet every mourner with a handshake before sitting barefoot on the floor with the other women. I listened wide-eyed. I asked when I should share comfort. Was there a program? How would we know what to do? When should we sing? Should we take something? What would be expected of Pastor Chambers? My "funeral lesson" was thorough, and every detail was noted in my mind.

The next day, Jim bought 25kg of mealie-meal as a token gift of care from the Bible Institute and missionary team while we shopped for chitenges for the girls and me. Banda pressed our new wardrobes and seemed quietly amused as we struggled to put them on. How in the world were we supposed to move in these "binders" without losing them! The Zambian women looked so natural in them. Me? I was not built with their proportions: I had hips! What was I to do with all this fabric bunched at my waist? I felt like I was dressed for a gunny sack race, only I wasn't allowed to hold onto the edges at the top. I begged Banda to show me how to do this, to demonstrate on himself.

In perfect Zambian courtesy Banda obliged my request, albeit reluctantly. If black skin could blush, his did. "Start from the back. The pattern on the material should be centered from the back." He turned around to show us, holding the two-meter cloth straight out and untied. "Then you bring the left side in first and tuck it in while the right side comes over. If you are thin enough, you can even tie one end to the other." I wasn't thin, but I was desperate. I tried to stretch cotton to new dimensions in an effort to prevent any unnecessary embarrassment of it falling off. Cotton doesn't stretch. I then shuffled my way back to the bedroom to put on my head scarf (the chitembala). A once-over look in the mirror convinced me that I resembled a gypsy ready for a costume party. Shuffling back down the hall, the chitenge loosened and then fell off. I grabbed the straying fabric and re-wrapped it extra tightly. Jim was calling that it was time to leave NOW! I asked Banda how I looked, and he said, "Fine." But that didn't mean a thing; everything was "fine" in Zambia.

The two older girls and I struggled a little bit to step up into the van with our binders. Once in, I waved a thumbs-up to Banda which meant I was still "together" in my new garb. He was holding Rebecca and Mary in the doorway, both of whom were unhappy to be left behind. Nathan ran to open the gate, and I gave him a look that said, "Pray!" I really did want to minister to people's hearts today, and not concentrate on my clothing. I was most grateful for the skirt underneath it!

As we drove, I reviewed all the tips and protocol that Banda had given me. Jim was more absorbed in driving and preparing his own thoughts, but the girls were obviously taking note of all I said, asking questions which came to mind. This first day of the funeral would be a critical time for comfort and tender care to the closest of kin; the day of burial would be a time for us to focus on encouraging the family through the final steps, and challenging those who are left. We wanted to communicate Christ in everything, even if the language we now spoke was not their own.

When we arrived at the house, we were instantly in the spotlight. Not many whites came to the African funerals. Some viewed us with curiosity; some with skepticism, some with open appreciation and respect. Jim carried the 25kg bag of mealie-meal to the women around the cooking fires, and I followed with a bag of tomatoes, onions, and cabbages. One woman seemed to respond to our English, so I introduced myself and explained that these gifts were from the missionaries and Bible Institute teachers. She and the other women seemed most appreciative, as it was their responsibility to feed all the gathering friends and relatives. The gifts broke the first, awkward barrier. She introduced herself as Sophie, Jazzy's aunt. I relaxed.

The girls and I hung tightly together, not sure where to go from there. While I had someone to talk with, they did not. I encouraged them to greet people as I inquired about the best time to share our songs. Sophie explained to Jim and I that all the family had not arrived yet, so the time for the burial could not be announced until Jazzy's father and stepmother came from their village. Apparently it was quite a remote place. News of Jazzy's passing had reached them, but they had to come by train, and this was quite a journey. Someone had telephoned that the parents should be expected that day.

After Sophie organized the food with the cooks, she introduced Jim to some of the men and took me by the hand to the house of mourning. The doorway was cluttered with an assortment of shoes, mostly flip-flops and plastic, black shoes. I removed my own sandals and added them to the collection as I entered the dark room. Once my eyes adjusted, I could see women sitting on the floor, a closed coffin and grass mats on the floor. The furniture had been removed to the outside where the men and children gathered. A few neighborhood women had entered ahead of us, sending up a fresh volley of wailing and chanting—sorrowful phrases which I did not understand, something like "ah-tah-tahh" and "Moo-loon-goo." Some were moaning softly; some simply sat unemotionally. The women who entered before us were on their knees, "walking" from person to person, shaking their hands and greeting each one. The birth mother of Jazzy was sitting near an empty coffin, wailing and rocking back and forth. She only stopped to wipe her face and nose with her chitenge.

I dropped to my knees and held out my hand to the first woman. She took it and responded with her eyes, especially when I greeted her softly in Nyanja. Each woman gave some quiet assent or communicated acceptance as I made my way around the room. When I came to the mother of Jazzy, my own heart just gave way, leaking out my eyes. She was a woman so filled with grief, and apparently so engrossed in her personal loss that the truth of Jazzy's eternal life in Christ had not curbed her sorrow. Maybe she did not know of it. My heart went out to her through both my hands as I clasped hers. Sophie was still in the room, so I motioned for her to come and translate for me. My consolation was brief, but genuine. I told her that I was sorry; that even though her son was not with HER, he was with Jesus, His Savior. He was going to be all right with Jesus, I was sure of it. She softened some, and I felt like I had connected in truth that I cared deeply.

After finishing my round of greetings, Sophie introduced me to the women. They made a spot for me next to the wall, opposite the doorway. Through the opening, I could see the cooking fires and much of the yard from there, including Jim and the girls. The wailing died down inside the house, and soft conversations took over, but not with the mother beside the coffin. Her grief seemed deep and prolonged. I longed to say something, but what would be understood in a room where English was not spoken?

As I was pondering and praying over when and what to share, a piercing death wail was heard outside. It sounded like someone had been stabbed. Inward alarm surfaced, and I am sure my face must have shown it, but no one in the room was moved to their feet, so I too, remained in my place of mourning against the wall. I had full view, however, of the yard through the open doorway. The loud shrieks, ugly and desperate, came closer, until I could at last view the person who uttered them. She was small in frame, older, and yet agile. She stumbled into the midst of the funeral yard throwing dust and wailing. Suddenly she cast herself on the ground before all in what looked to me like a seizure, with convulsions of grief and a torrent of words I could not understand. It was unrelenting and extreme. I felt someone needed to go and help her, but I was pinned to the wall with protocol and my own inexperience. I could only watch through the doorway.

The women next to me were also watching through the doorway, as were those seated in the yard. In the background, I could see someone leading an old man by the hand. He lurched heavily into the chair he was offered, and stared ahead dully, ignoring the woman in the dust entirely. I did not think it polite to stare, so I glanced around the room to see if any were moved by these new visitors. The women seemed to be listening with one ear, but accepting of it. Meanwhile, the woman on the ground writhed, gaining momentum in her crying and confusing behavior. She beat the ground hysterically, almost angrily. White foam began coming out her mouth, as she babbled and shrieked and thrashed about. I was sure this was an epileptic seizure.

"Is she all right?" I whispered to Sophie. "She has stuff coming out of her mouth. Who is she?"

"She is the second wife of the father to Jazzy. They have just come from the village and she is just showing their grief," she explained. She could see the alarm and discomfort in my eyes as I watched.

My thoughts were half-prayers mixed with deep sorrow. This woman would not put on this display of extreme hopelessness if she only knew what Jazzy was experiencing right now. I wondered if he could even see it from heaven; I didn't know. A couple more women came to the doorway, took off their shoes, and sent up loud cries. This signaled all the other women to weep afresh, particularly the mother sitting beside the coffin. The room was a cacophony of sorrow. I was overwhelmed. I cried at the despair around me. I could only think "weep with those who weep," but in my heart, I determined that I must tell them the truth about Jazzy. I must! The truth would surely comfort, I reasoned.

Perhaps twenty to thirty more minutes passed. Someone had picked up the woman in the yard, and again the room quieted down. This was the moment I had waited for. I whispered to Sophie, "Do you think I could be given the chance to say something to the women?" Her response was to hush the women. "And would you translate for me?" She raised her eyebrows in assent. Every woman's eye was upon me except the mother's. The moment was intense for me. I thought a single-line prayer to the Lord and sighed from my soul.

I cannot remember the exact words, as if to quote them verbatim, but I remember the gist. I spoke of hope. It was so needful to comfort them with the certainty that Jazzy had been saved from permanent separation from God. I reviewed his testimony of trusting Christ in life and in death. I spoke of the place he now was, the place Christ has prepared for him ahead of this day. I spoke of the freedom at death; God's condemning judgment would not be what he faced, but rather forgiveness and mercy. All the ears and eyes focused on what I said. Some were confirming my words with nods and affirming sounds.

I felt like I had connected, or God had. Some thanked me in Nyanja, but I was most encouraged that the mother seemed more peaceful, though heavy with grief.

Outside, I could see Jim and the girls waiting for me. Jim motioned that it was time for us to sing, so as soon as some of the women left the house, I followed on my knees to the doorway. There, I stood to my feet and found my sandals. My chitenge had come loose with all the sitting and crawling, making it necessary for me to grasp it with one hand while walking. Sophie noticed my dilemma, asking if I wanted some help. I gushed out a "please!" and she secured it for me, showing me how to tie a "cheater's knot" at one end to hold it in place. I asked her about the woman who'd come in throwing dust. She explained further that Jazzy's parents had divorced a long time ago, and his mother had remained in the city. The father was the witchdoctor in the village. In my heart, I wondered if this display of bizarre behavior was demonic possession. I'd never seen anything like it before; that was for sure.

Megan, Anne, and I were introduced to those seated in the yard— mostly men. We greeted them all. The stepmother sat quietly by herself in the shade. Her husband remained in a stupor on his chair. We sang songs of friendship in and beyond this life: "What A Friend We Have In Jesus," "There's Not A Friend Like the Lowly Jesus," and "Amazing Grace." As the three-part harmony reached the ears of the women in the house, they came out of the doorway to listen and enjoy. The music drew even more from the neighborhood, so that when we were finished, the yard had filled. It was then Jim's turn to speak. He spoke about a Friend who sticks closer than a brother, even through death. The people were warm and attentive. Our acceptance was evident.

The next day, Wednesday, was the burial day and we ministered again, briefly this time. We arrived in the morning to be with the family and funeral procession. The men who were to prepare the body left for the mortuary at the hospital, and the remaining mourners waited patiently for the transportation to arrive for the trip to the cemetery. Other than getting occasional glances at my chitenge, I felt like we were not the spectacle that we had been yesterday. Something was not quite right, but of course no one would come right out and say it. Some even made comments of appreciation that we were there, that we had sung, and that we brought the food. Sophie made a point of introducing Jim and me, explaining our role in Jazzy's life and our part in the funeral. Meanwhile, Steve and Ruth Ann arrived in their big, green truck. They would be driving and Steve—who knew Jazzy better and longer than the rest of us missionaries—would speak at the gravesite.

Waiting for the arrival of the body was always unpredictable. No one could know how quickly the body would be released or how long the lines at the mortuary would be. When it finally did arrive, loud wailing resumed, and fresh grief surfaced, particularly among the family. The closest of kin were given the choice of riding in the back of the truck next to the coffin, or inside a vehicle. The mother stayed right next to the casket, mourning with heaviness and fatigue. The father was dark and silent; the stepmother was completely worn out, sitting without conversation or companionship.

As soon as the funeral procession rolled onto the dirt street, the mourners began singing. Beautiful harmonies in traditional languages filled the air, and my heart. We followed the truck, trying to take in the experience: new sounds; new protocol in death; the people; the sadness of it all. Our own van was filled with mourners, so Jim and I could not converse much, even though we were sitting right next to each other in the front seat. I didn't feel like talking anyway. It was not a time to analyze, but rather a time to respect.

About twenty minutes later, we turned off the main road into the city cemetery. The traffic back-logged at the entrance, as multiple funeral processions waited for each other to pass on the rugged inner roads. Graves and headstones numbered in the thousands and stretched farther than my eyes could see, it was larger than Arlington cemetery, and far less kempt. Our van lurched on the mud-rutted roads, passing more graves, trucks and busses parked alongside the roads. We were in a virtual sea of graves.

We stopped at a small, cement-block pavilion, waiting our turn for the body viewing. The pavilion was divided by a partial wall to allow for two funeral processions at the same time. We still had to wait in the scorching sun until it was our turn. The pallbearers carried the casket to the cement bench and opened the top portion for viewing. Mourners were then told to form a queue. Some walked past the body with simple glances, as if they almost denied the reality; others were hysterical, falling or swooning in front of the casket; still others, exhausted and hoarse from continual crying, moaned or shrieked out pitiful words of farewell. The sting of death was real.

Jim placed his hand on my back to lead me into the procession. I actually was dreading seeing Jazzy like this. As we drew nearer, I could not recognize him. Apparently, the time in the sun, lack of embalming, and four days post-death had caused bloating in his features. I felt embarrassed for him. I took one last look, wishing I could just remember him as he was in Bible School, wishing I could just go back and start all over from the phone call at Lusaka Hotel. But death has no reverse.

After the last mourners, the parents, and the family, had gone through the line, the casket was returned to the truck, and we were again pitching in the sea of graves. The burial site was quite a distance from the viewing pavilion, so we were impressed yet once more with field after field of graves—some freshly dug, some overgrown with weeds. It all signaled pandemic death.

When we arrived at the gravesite, there were multiple open graves nearby, each numbered. The death certificate and papers told where the body was to be placed. Other burials were in process around us, so there was a cacophony of choirs, weeping, preaching, and individual conversations. The grave had to be measured for depth and length. Someone eyeballed a dry stick that seemed to be about right, and measured the casket, grave depth, and sides from that. Then two pallbearers began shoveling more dirt from the depth and sides of the grave to the mound beside it. When one tired, another took over.

When they were finished, one man took a shovel of dirt from the mound, and seemed to offer it to each individual family member, seated on the ground nearby. One by one they touched it with their fingertips. It must have meant something, but we would have to ask about it later. The men now moved to place the casket into the grave, followed by refilling the grave with dirt from the mound. Dust filled the air. A mound now began to form over the hole. The men beat it with the backs of their shovels until it was firm. While all this was happening, the Bible school students, the believers, and Ruth Ann and I joined in singing hymns from the Nyanja songbook.

A man from the family stood at the head of the grave. He thanked everyone for coming, read a eulogy, and introduced Steve. Though I did not ask, it seemed that this was a particularly emotional time for him. He had led Jazzy to Christ when he first came into Zambia. I prayed for him to get through it, both emotionally and physically, since the heat was oppressive.

The last part of the service was the wreath laying. The man who read the eulogy began to call out names of funeral guests and family members. As each name was called, the party would go to the mound and lay flowers or a simple wreath, embedding some part of it into the dirt to secure it. Some were demonstrative with grief and goodbyes to Jazzy; some, simply respectful. When our names were called, I simply imitated what I saw others do. Jim and I knelt at the mound in respect, and then placed the flower into the fresh dirt mound. As I returned to my spot, I again caught some of the women's eyes. They were amused at my chitenge for some reason. It was of no consequence, but I was already feeling threatened by self-consciousness.

A prayer closed the burial service, and everyone dispersed to the cars. The trucks and vans filled again to return to the funeral house for a final meal. The family would remain for several days to determine the future of Jazzy's belongings and his children. We were told that the children were to be sent back to the village with his father, the witch-doctor and the stepmother. I groaned in my spirit, wondering about their future, crying out to God for them. I would cry out in prayer for weeks to come. I wish I could take them and add them to our clan, unrealistic as it was.

After returning our passengers to the funeral house, we were invited to share in the meal which followed. A large basin of clean water was placed at the entrance to the yard for everyone to wash their hands and face as we came into the yard. We simply followed others' lead, and were soon offered some meat and nshima inside one of the rooms of the house. As we ate, we could see the pleasure of the people. We enjoyed being part of them, and they of us. We could not linger though. We were to leave for a mini vacation with the Fogles, Sherry, and Doreen that afternoon; so we made our farewell rounds as graciously as was appropriate and left for home. I wished I had known why my chitenge caught the attention of the women. It was only many months and many funerals later that I learned how out of style and custom I was: this was Indian fabric (not cool) rather than African!

This funeral—one of hundreds to come—made a permanent mark on my heart. I had witnessed the sting of death in its unmasked form, with no anesthesia. The grave had swallowed thousands already. The hopeless witchdoctor and his wife and Jazzy's children remained in my heart—to burden it and to benefit it. They reminded me of the sting of death: the after effects of poisonous lies that bite and kill hope of eternal life in Christ. If there were to be any balm for it, I had to think and speak about real Life after all this sorrow—the delight of being resurrected with a new body, of a new and eternal life with God. I also wanted to learn from The Man of Sorrows, for I would be well acquainted with grief in this place, even as He.

* * *

"As a follower of Jesus Christ, you have been called by God...
Not to live out a perfect life in your own perfect little corner
of the world, But to come alongside imperfect people suffering
the inevitable pain of living in an imperfect world."[2]

Chapter 19

A Water Break

Our entire family had been on an emotional and spiritual marathon. The funeral was only one small leg of the race. We'd crossed rugged terrain of change ever since arriving, not to mention crossing the cliff hangers of the soul—like the abandonment of all we knew to be home. Fortunately, our family ran as a pack, but every single individual felt the personal wear and tear on the soul as we pounded down a bumpy, cross-cultural road. Every day held some sort of step-by-step challenge, and every day each individual in the family had to determine how he or she would put the next foot down. Facing those decisions can be stressful, and that stress, cumulative. We were at a point in April that we needed to take a breather from the race. Our nerves—on overload—were screaming for some time off, some fun!

A trip to Victoria Falls had been planned with the Fogles, Sherry, and Doreen. It just happened that Jazzy's funeral delayed our intentions by two days. We were more ready than ever for a change of mood and atmosphere, and Nathan's sixteenth birthday was the perfect time to do it. The Falls, six hours from the capital, was one of the grandest spots on the earth to commemorate this milestone. He was excited about that, as we all were.

Getting the car packed after the funeral was relatively smooth. The three oldest kids could be very efficient, particularly when energized by adrenaline rushes and a break from the routines. We were supposed to leave by one o'clock so that we could arrive in Livingstone before dark.

It simply was too dangerous to travel at night in Africa, and the road had its own hazards, even in daylight: potholes, unmarked edges, and untrained drivers. Since the funeral delayed our departure a bit, we began our venture under some pressure. After meeting up with the Fogles and the ladies, we juggled passengers and belongings according to space and convenience. Alex, our night guard and translator, was also coming along for this premiere display.

It took about twenty minutes to reach the main road leading out of the city, and for some reason, we had to stop. I think Larry wanted to price heaps of stones there for a building project. We let the children out to wiggle or to barter with the Zambian sellers next to the road while they waited. During the course of this, Janine Fogle's change purse came up missing; no matter how many times she retraced her steps, she could not find it. It was apparent that someone had stolen it. Larry questioned the stone sellers thoroughly, but got nowhere. Alex knew better. He pressed one particular woman over and over to return it. The conversation became louder, each person becoming more insistent and convincing of his or her side.

Meanwhile, I went back to the van. My nerves were so tired, and I was so impatient! I was somewhere between praying and aggravated reasoning. "Why can't something go right, for once? Why can't we just have ONE, happy outing without continual problems? God, would you do something?" I didn't know what, but this was so characteristic of life lately! "Problems, problems, problems!" I had had it, I thought. I pleaded with God to get us on the road again; the pressure of darkness was before us. God is so merciful to me! The woman reluctantly dug deep into the stone pile and uncovered Janine's missing purse. I was shocked! We'd won! Now that didn't happen often.

The delay was unavoidable. I wished my nerves had not been so over-taxed. It was harder to FEEL patient or spiritual or anything good in my state of mind. Even small things were getting to me, ready to fester—like a splinter under a fingernail. Once we were on the road again, my mood calmed down, and the excitement of the trip resumed.

I glanced back at the children. They seemed unaffected. The farther we drove out of the city, the more distance I put between myself and the aggravations. I was just beginning to feel victorious—for about an hour and a half, that is—when the car began to clatter. It had no power when we tried to accelerate. Jim pulled off the side of the road, and Larry's van followed. My sense of "spirituality" dropped back down several points. My Self kicked in some worthless comment about "this stupid car."

Jim's head went into Tin Lizzy's innards. Nathan and Larry watched the car doctor. I was anxious, casting glances at the sun and at my watch. I knew we were going to be driving in the dark at this rate. I tried to distract myself from worry by talking to others in Larry's van. Sallie's calm demeanor warded off the returning aggravations and unspoken tension I felt. Before long, Jim's head emerged, announcing that the lifters had shaken loose. Whatever! It was fixable. He thought we should be fine now.

Back on the road, we drove another half hour before a new problem developed. The transmission seal was leaking oil, and Jim could not repair it there on the road. We had to pull over several times to check the oil and keep the engine cool. By this time, the sun was threateningly low in the sky. We were in the middle of nowhere, and still going the speed of a golf cart. I was trying to control the internal combustion going on inside me. I glanced back at the kids. Nathan was quiet. That was not normal. He seemed to be dealing with his own internal affairs. I took note. This stuff could really get to you.

I asked Jim in my worry voice, "What are we going to do? It's getting dark."

Jim's response more than hinted at his own frustration and tension. There was nothing to do but continue slowly down the road until we reached the next town—Monze. Having no real experience outside Lusaka, we were left to imagine what others defined as "unsafe" after dark. I really did not want to find out, and my imagination was altogether too vivid already. I prayed intensely that God would get all of us to this "Monze" safely, before the oil ran completely out and spoiled the new engine and our getaway. I also prayed for whatever was bugging Nathan. He wasn't really himself. He was more like a punctured ball that would not bounce.

"Before they call, I will answer; and while they are still speaking, I will hear."[1] God was there with us, chugging along in the van. He was there when I was more obsessed with the time and the problems and us, than with His capability to help. Even more amazing, He helped us. He pushed us into Monze just as the last rays of light were leaving the sky. A few curious pedestrians watched our entourage limp in and park at a gas station on the edge of town. The men made a few inquiries about night accommodations and possibilities for the van to be repaired the next day. We were directed to the town's hotel, not far from the main road. It was our only option, particularly at this hour.

To say who was more intrigued by this visitation, the Americans or the Zambians, would be hard to guess. This hotel was clearly run by Zambians, for Zambians, so when fifteen Americans and Alex stood at the check-in, bags in hand, one can only imagine the looks and whispers circulating on both sides. I stood there, a bedraggled soul in a bedraggled atmosphere, sizing up the patchwork of tiles on the floor and the "vintage" curtains at the window. It was obviously a mix and match of whatever was either free or available to the proprietor. Since the spirit of the hotel seemed rather eclectic, we also combined kids as could be accommodated by the hotel, grateful for a place to lay our heads down.

I entered our room and switched on the light. A bare bulb shown over the tile floor: green, gold, white, beige tiles filled in spaces, while a few remained missing—like teeth in a smile. Two sets of striped curtains hung about one foot short of reaching the sill, exposing us to the onlookers from the alley and the tavern next door. Privacy was clearly going to be a problem. A quick survey of the bathroom: black and grey tiles on the floor; an old porcelain bathtub with an eternal stream coming from the faucet; two, very third-world-looking towels; and—what was this?—a telephone wire coming from the top of the commode tank! That deserved further investigation, later. I returned to the bedroom to deposit my belongings and then leave again for supper.

We walked down a dark, chocolate-brown hallway to an empty dining area. Everyone was famished and chatty, ready to make the evening meal the night's social event. The kitchen staff, however, was not as prepared for that. The menu was written on cardboard, but the waiter informed us that tonight's menu was a choice between beef stew and chicken curry, and there was only one soft drink available—orange Fanta. That simplified the ordering process and refined the appetites. Remembrances of our Kafue river escapade resurfaced, renewing a lust for an adventure. Humor returned to my soul, and others' in spite of our fatigue.

After supper, we headed for our rooms and prepared for bed. I walked into the bathroom to freshen up. The stream in the tub could not be remedied: the faucet was stripped out. No wash cloths. Ok, I would use one of my socks. As for the toilet, the flush knob hung limply towards the floor. A hole had been drilled into the top of the tank. The phone wire attached to the inner gizmo which released water from the tank to the bowl. I pulled it to see if it worked. This only added to my adventure. I dressed for bed in the bathroom, and asked Jim if it was safe to return to the bedroom. Interpretation: had he found a remedy for lengthening the window treatments? The height of the top rod was beyond his reach, and nothing was long enough other than the sheet—which we needed for the night.

Jim changed Rebecca and laid her down on her baby blanket next to the wall, surrounded by our suitcases. He then took his turn in the bath/dressing room and I put Rebecca to sleep. When he returned, I pulled back the covers. A couple cockroaches scuttled across vintage sheets, manila colored from age. I quickly sucked in air. My consolation; cockroaches hate humans as much as humans hate cockroaches. We promised not to bother each other. My, was it something! I felt an adventure coming on.

I lay there in the dark, listening to the African rumba as I watched the beer signs flash off and on. I could pretend that the sound of running water from the tub was a fresh, country stream. I could pretend that the cockroaches had been crickets. The bed mattress surely gave me the hammock effect as I sunk deep into its springless bottom. But I could not think of one thing to make that music and the noise of drunken men fit into either an adventure or a dream. I did not sleep much or well. We moved Rebecca between us to protect her from our "cricket friends."

The next morning we all went down for breakfast. The cardboard box menu for the morning looked delicious: Danish, scones, biscuits, several egg choices, porridge, tea and juice. Larry organized our orders for efficiency and simplicity and motioned for the waiter. With over enunciation, he condensed the order, and even helped spell some of it for the man to write it down. Larry questioned him on whether he understood it all. He looked uncomfortable. The waiter assured Larry that he understood the order and disappeared behind the door to the kitchen.

We had plenty of time to talk in his thirty minute absence: we shared impressions of the tavern going until three in the morning, cockroach stories, and such. Nathan said Alex got very excited over using their bath tub. He raved about having soap, too. That seemed to put into perspective our different expectations, as well as the meaning of gratitude. After forty-five minutes, Larry signaled for the waiter, asking whether our food was ready. The waiter assured us it was coming.

About ten minutes later, out came two bowls of biscuits, a juice drink, and several egg orders. Then, nothing more. Those already served were polite, but their food was getting cold. Again, Larry called the waiter to get an explanation. Jim needed to get the van to a garage for repairs, so we did not want to continue waiting to eat. Larry asked about the rest of the order. The waiter politely smiled, but did not give any direct answers. Larry asked where the Danish rolls were. The waiter pointed with his eyes at the bowl of biscuits.

"Oh! That's a Danish?" Larry queried. There were others at the table chiming in like echoes.

"Yes," he replied.

"So where's the scones. We had five who ordered scones."

The waiter pointed to the other bowl.

"So those are scones?"

"Yes."

"But those in that bowl are the same as what is in this bowl." Larry said. Everyone supported him with our inquisitive looks.

"Yes," the waiter repeated.

"But which is it, Danish or scones?"

"Yes," was again the response. The waiter looked uncomfortable. Larry pressed him several times for clarity: was the bowl full of biscuits, scones, or Danish? Each reply was affirmative. Larry then interpreted what we all knew, this was all we were getting, because this is all there was. Then Larry repeated the order, noting that toast had not yet appeared, and some had still not received their egg orders. The waiter disappeared again into the kitchen. When he returned about ten minutes later, he made a simple statement. "We have twelve eggs."

"You mean you only have twelve eggs? But we have fifteen people!" was the response. "You took our order!" The poor waiter looked distressed. "Can you get more?" Larry asked.

"Eggs are finished." was his uneasy response. It was clear we were making one another feel ill at ease, so Larry thanked him. At least there was plenty of tea. We polished off the "Danish/scones/biscuits" and checked out of the hotel, heading for the garage. I pulled out some peanut butter and snacks for myself, Alex, and others not yet fed. I asked myself what in the world all that was about. If they didn't have something, why didn't they just tell you so you could adjust to it? When in the world would I understand and APPRECIATE this indirect approach to communicating? Well, meanwhile, it was worth laughing over, so we did.

The van repairs took most of the morning. It gave everyone a chance to explore the shops and observe the small-town life of Africa. I watched people with fascination, intrigued by the women who carried most of their lives on their heads or on their backs; the oxen and carts; the bicycles; the cultural warmth of smiles and handshakes; and the fabulous display of color. This was not wasted time, even though it was a delay. I *loved* these scenes. This was an adventure!

Being back on the road was a blessing, even though the potholes jarred Tin Lizzy to her axles. We saw huts and lush woods along the road. Nathan sat behind me, taking it all in. He was quiet, thinking about something rather deeply. Three hours later, we were riding through rolling terrain. As we crested a hill, we saw in the distance, off to the right, what looked like a vast cloud of smoke billowing from the ground upward. It was actually the mist of Victoria Falls in peak performance. Excitement vibrated through the van.

Larry led the way to our night's accommodation: Rainbow Lodge, right on the Zambezi River. As soon as we arrived, the children spilled out gratefully while the adults unpacked the vans and checked us in. The chalets were round, white huts with thatched roofs, nicely arranged within. Monkeys scampered on the grounds among the chalets, or swung playfully in the trees. One was particularly curious about Aimee Fogle's ivory ring, and tried to snatch it for himself. This kept the children's keen interest. It was perfect. My heart sighed relief at last. I felt like a tourist on a getaway.

The older children investigated the river, the monkeys, and the trail to the Falls. They came back announcing that we could not see them that night because it was dusk. This was just enough time for Sherry to discover that her chalet had no water. Reporting it at the desk, we were told there was a problem. No one had water. Maybe we would like to have supper first, while they worked on it. That sounded great!

We chose to eat right on the bank of the Zambezi, in a thatched pavilion. There were actual menus at this place and two kinds of soft drinks: Coke and Fanta. The waiter was fluent in English, professionally dressed, and could write quickly. We placed our orders and waited.

Larry's fish arrived on a platter, head, tail, scales, and eyeballs. This sight awakened Larry's crazy side. He picked up the entire fish, and held it before him, eyeball to eyeball. Then he pretended they were kissing each other. Other customers accepted our weirdness playfully, understanding our attempt to cope with the mishaps and mystique of Africa.

The next day was our first exposure to Victoria Falls. We paid the 500 kwacha per person, about a quarter, and set out on the trail. The first sight of this mile-wide cascade was overwhelming. We could not take it in for magnitude or majesty. The water plummeted over a four hundred and twenty foot drop with such force that we could not comprehend it. In some places we could not see the other side, and with the mist we could not get as much as a glimpse of the bottom. It was gloriously impossible! The roar of it deafened us to our own voices. The African name was quite descriptive of this phenomenon: Musi-o-tunya, the Smoke That Thunders. A continual rainstorm, created by the billowing mist and spray, drenched and invigorated us.

Alex stood in awe, his eyes full of wonder and near-disbelief. "God is so great! God is so great!" He repeated himself several times. "How could anyone say there is no God!" He shouted above the roar, shaking his head in denial that anyone could overlook the existence of the Sovereign Power behind this. The Falls were shouting, "ever since the creation of the world His invisible nature and attributes, that is His eternal power and divinity have been made intelligible and clearly discernible in and through the things that have been made..so men are without excuse."[2]

Nathan asked permission to leave the rest of us and go on his own. In respect of his sixteenth birthday, we encouraged him with simple cautions for safety. There were no guardrails in places along the ridge, so one careless slip would be certain death. The danger, though, only added to the man-sized adventure he needed that day. A man-sized heart was developing inside that chest.

We walked with the little girls and Micah in hand. The older girls were on their own with the Fogles. Nathan distanced himself from us, and I had to commit him to God. I prayed for him right then, that whatever he needed, God would address. The next time we saw him, he was flat on his belly, with his head peering right over the very edge of the chasm. The mist billowed up, and the "rain" from the up-spray came in torrents. He was transfixed. I wished I could read his thoughts. Jim told me to leave him alone, so I did, even though my instincts were insecure about his precarious position.

We worked our way through the rainforest and trees, coming to a narrow footbridge which spanned part of the canyon. There we crossed onto an island, even further into the canyon. A torrential blast of water and wind blew the spray wildly into our faces. My soul could not get enough of this. It was cleansing. It was perspective to one whose joy had dehydrated in the heat of trials. I did not know which divine attributes were revealed to others by this nature display, but God the Spirit spoke to me of His overwhelming power and presence. I could not stand in this turbulent wonder—drenched by it, blown by it, awed by it, frightened by it—and just ignore it. It was impossible! The experience took over of its own magnitude. Even so, standing in God's presence and before His power was to be reckoned with. One day every person on earth would be overcome by the experience and magnitude of His Presence. Everyone would fall on his knees in fear and awe and silent wonder. Right then, I was in wordless worship.

There was nothing to rush us—no tour guide or rules beyond common sense. We absorbed the sight and sound of God's masterpiece uninhibited. As we circled back from the island to the footbridge, two sights delighted me. One, a double rainbow arched over the water beyond the footbridge...I'd never seen one before. And a second thrill, just like that double rainbow, met my eyes. Nathan and the kids were squealing their pleasure above the roar of the water, hydroplaning on Knifeback Bridge. There was NOTHING somber or reserved anymore; they were extracting every ounce of wildness available from the moment. There was no reservation in their joy. I stood there to soak in my amazement.

When we all returned to the parking lot, not one thread nor hair was dry, and nobody cared. Nathan ran up the steps and over to Jim and me. He threw his wet arms around me and then Jim in a long, soppy hug. "Mom! Dad! God is so AWESOME!" All his enthusiasm was back. I looked at him with wonder, having had my own version of the experience with the same conclusion. We hugged back.

My eyes questioned him. "Did you get things sorted out?" My mother-tone was taking over. "What's been bothering you, Nathan?"

Nathan looked at Jim and me straight from his heart. "Oh... I've been so depressed 'cause I turned sixteen, and I can't get my license. All my friends are getting theirs. But this is so much more awesome than driving a car!" All of a sudden, I understood what all the broodings meant. A piece of manhood was in that license. Nathan took off with renewed gusto.

My heart did cartwheels. Only God could really meet Nathan's needs; only God knew what makes a real man, a fulfilled man. As parents, we wanted everything to be "right" for our kids; we wanted to fix their problems, give them a normal life and their rights. We tended to assume these would bring them happiness. God, on the other hand, wanted Nathan to discover *Himself*, and in that, find satisfaction. We could never have taught satisfaction to Nathan in devotions or Bible class. It had to be understood as he lived it out himself. "Your faithfulness endures to *all generations*."[3]

The car was filled with chatter as we returned to Rainbow Lodge to change into dry clothes. It was recommended that we switch hotels, since there did not seem to be a remedy in sight for the water situation, and the monkey business was a little out of hand. Monkeys can get pesky and somewhat threatening. These seemed such little things, now that we had washed our souls seven times in the Zambezi. Perspective had been restored.

We loaded into the vans and headed for the edge of town to find the Fairmont Hotel. It was an old colonial looking building, beautifully white with a lovely screen awning over the car park in front. We remained in the cars while the men went in to inquire about rooms. A man in his thirties came walking up with a bucket and dirty rag, asking if he could wash our van. Someone in the van advised me to not to accept because we would be forced to pay. So, I politely explained we did not want the car washed. He wouldn't accept my refusal; I would not accept his. After several rounds of this, he simply began washing it anyway. I warned him that we would not pay. Even Alex, in his own language, could not persuade him to leave it alone. By the time Jim and Larry returned, both vans were sparkling. Now the man expected to be paid, obligating us to him. Jim and Larry refused. The man became indignant, and then violent, demanding loudly that we pay him for his work. It was clear he wanted to make a spectacle of us. That, he did!

Jim does not get bullied easily. He let the man know we had not agreed to it, and that brought a fresh volley of anger and curses in the man's mother tongue. Alex looked embarrassed, saying that was bad; very, very bad. We asked him what was said. He said he had put a curse upon us. The devil would be taking us to hell. We'd never been cursed before, but we have a Perfect Shield for such times. We drove off, a little unnerved, but definitely not to hell. I prayed for the man.

The rest of the trip was adventurous, but even the game drive paled in splendor to the wonder of Victoria Falls. In the seventeen years since then, I cannot recall one year when the Falls has been so full or so beautiful. Nor can I remember it filling my soul and spirit as much as it did that year.

* * *

"The Lord on high is mightier than the noise of many waters."[4]

Chapter 20

A Woman Goes Fishing

Having returned with a fresh outlook, I felt renewed in my vision to reach out within the neighborhood of Chilenge. There were no believing women in the church that I could tell. Several attended regularly, calling themselves members, but there was no evidence that God lived within them. Some were certainly morally good and lovely women, but they lacked an understanding or a hunger for spiritual things. They sat through lessons and preaching with polite disinterest, as if fulfilling a checklist of respectable duties. Some had a mild but genuine curiosity about salvation from sinfulness, but lacked honesty to address it in their personal lives. Most of the women of the neighborhood avoided our little house church. The neighborhood was strongly Catholic, and we had little history or credibility in the community at that point.

I assessed the situation and took a deep breath. I was going to have to get into the heart and homes of women in this community. I hardly knew where to begin. I never was a natural at witnessing. I always seemed to go too deep, too soon, or too cerebral, or else couldn't find a way to begin a spiritual conversation at all! In short, I knew I didn't have the "gift" of evangelism, but I could not get beyond the fact that I had a responsibility to do it. Furthermore, the chasm of culture and language was broad and looming, and my little rope bridge to others swung precariously when I walked into people's lives.

This is where the reality of Jesus Christ met with the truth about me. I could imagine God being irritated, "What is your big problem? You ought to know what you are doing by now." Well, I didn't, but I wanted to! But imagination was not truth. I had a letter from God that told me a few things. It assured me that He wasn't impatiently thumping His fingers in the sky over my learning disabilities. It revealed that He was touched with the feelings of my weaknesses. It told me that I was not the first to struggle with being a witness for Him. God had given me a promise in writing: "I will make you become fishers of [wo]men…"[1] That was the key: becoming. And Christ, the Master Fisherman, would teach me.

I began to fish with one desire—reeling in relationships. My past experiences confirmed to me that talking had little permanent impact without a relationship to give words meaning. So, I began to think of ways to catch the women's attention. In the next several months, I found three ways: home visits, tea parties, and the Zambian cuisine.

Jim and I set aside two days each week to build relationships in the community. For one or two hours of those days, we would walk the dirt streets of Chilenge, becoming familiar with the faces and personalities of the neighborhood. Sometimes conversations opened into matters of the heart and spirit; sometimes they were simply connections for us, invitations into their homes and then their lives. Becoming familiar in the neighborhood was like throwing the fishing line into the water. We first became a curiosity, then a common sight and then a new relationship latched on. Both Jim and I struggled with ourselves—to feel at ease at first, but we really loved it. In fact, it challenged and invigorated us!

As I became acquainted with the many streets, houses, and families, I realized that there weren't very many limitations on the word "all" in 1 Corinthians 9:22: "I have become all things to all men…" (NKJV). One hot day I was walking through the dirt streets of Chilenje and passed the yard of a family whose reputation lacked respect. My eye caught a glimpse of a limp and emaciated young woman. She was warming herself in the sun, her eyes were closed and her head flopped heavily to one side in sleep. The protruding bones in her face and body signaled her diseased condition. This was one of THEM, I told myself—one of the twenty-five percent with you-know-what. The Spirit prompted me to go to her. I reminded myself to obey, even though I felt completely inadequate to know where or how to hook into a conversation.

"Hello?" I greeted her. "How are you?" I said with concern.

Her eyes squinted in the sun. "Fine, but not so fine," Her voice flat lined. "I'm sick."

I nodded. "I see that. I was just passing by and wondered if I could do anything to help you. I'm a missionary."

We exchanged names, and I tried to lead the conversation toward the Lord, but her attention span was short. She said she needed to sleep. Her labored breathing and skeletal features confirmed her need for rest, for help. There was no beauty left to her face, no charm or personality to draw me in, no health and no money. There she sat —without God and without hope. My heart went out to her. I left her with tracts, prayed with her, and promised to return.

Outside her gate, I took a deep breath. I had to change. I had to become ALL THINGS, even to identify with disease and death "that I might by all means save some."[2] My very sheltered background had actually avoided people like this, and maybe subconsciously disdained them. I was still afraid of them, afraid of "getting what they had." How could I "fish" for what I rejected? It was a spiritual oxymoron. I felt like I was sticking the wrong end of the pole into the water; I would win no one to the Lord unless I humbled myself and became ALL things, even identifying with AIDS and loving sick "fish." This was troubling, challenging, but necessary.

In the weeks that followed, I continued to roam the streets of the community, but I visited this woman whenever I could. When she was worse, I felt worse. Instinctively, I found myself touching her arm or squeezing her hand—just wanting to be around her. God was amazing me. He was loving her, using my own two hands and heart to do it! When He said He loved the WORLD, He visualized people like this woman—people with reproach and disease and sin-laden bodies. I'd never visualized people like her because I had never associated with them or been their neighbor. "But God, who is rich in mercy"[3] did. He'd become human flesh and lived among "THEM." "THEY" were some of His neighbors—and now they were mine.

Over the months that followed, Jesus taught me to fish. I grew more at ease with this friend. We could talk about the Lord, about life, about her problems and cares and about the meaning of Christ's love. She asked questions. I answered what I could. One day He opened up her understanding of how deep and broad and high and far-reaching His love was towards her. Christ put upon Himself her sin, her disease, and all the punishment she rightly deserved. He made her a worthy person, His own child. She trusted Jesus Christ, and He gave her eternal life. I don't know who was happier—she, me, or the angels who were rejoicing over her. The day that she went to be with God forever, I was there, watching, amazed afresh at the grace of my God .

The church did not boom in attendance, but little by little, we were wading deeper into the real life of our attendees and those who were watching us. Now when we greeted one another, there was less formality or superficiality. Now we had something to talk about, like life and eternal things. I wanted more. I wanted them to come to my house. Believe it or not, I was ready for another tea party. It seemed like the bait that few women would turn down.

On visitation the next few weeks, I invited the ladies to my house. Maggie, Banda's daughter, invited four of her friends, and many of the people on the street where our house church was promised to come. Some gave "cultural yeses" which was a polite way to decline without being negative, but I felt certain that some would actually show up. I made a point of emphasizing the time to start. They all knew it was 9:00.

At 8:50 I was running around like a maniac, making sure every detail was in place. I had only one sheet cake this time, and the spiritual presentation was FIRST on the agenda. I didn't want it said that I never learned from my mistakes. I kept looking out the window, checking the gate to be sure no one was waiting out there. At 9:00, there was still no sign of women. Every five minutes or less, I checked the gate and then my watch. I was so disappointed; not one soul had shown up! At 9:40, I heard a knock at the gate. Maggie appeared with five other women, and each apologized kindly for being "a little bit late." I hurried them into the living room and after my inner anxiety lessened, I welcomed them even more genuinely.

We began with a fun game to loosen the atmosphere. They loved to laugh. I loved to see them laugh. At 9:55, Sophie and Sarah entered, quietly apologizing for being a little late. I tried to hide my reaction and get back into the swing of the game. At 10:15, Matilda and Aritha shuffled into the room. They cheerfully giggled about their time of arrival, saying insincerely, "Oh, sorry to be late." I was just as sincere at rolling my eyes behind my lids. By this time, I could see I needed to adjust the devotional time to the end, if I was going to get everyone involved. This "little bit late" had no boundaries! I gave in to the cultural norm and killed a little more time with the refreshments and tea. This time, I knew how to serve, and how much. I was having fun. By 10:25, everyone was in full swing, having a great time. Ten ladies had consumed an entire chocolate sheet cake and some cookies, but none looked sick yet. We were making progress.

My grand finale was my presentation—an introduction to our church, our beliefs and purpose for being in the neighborhood. This was my chance to share the great news of Jesus Christ's work and power over death and sin. I noticed that two women in particular kept their heads down, refusing eye contact. I asked for questions from the group, but was faced with polite smiles or blank expressions. I closed in prayer, and then handed out a hostess gift: tea towels with crocheted ends and matching hot pads. They loved them. I finished the party with a closing prayer just after 11:05. The women lingered, chatting happily with one another.

At 11:15, there was a knock at the gate. There stood one of the women I'd invited, her baby tied on her back. Her clothing was clean, but holey and faded. My heart went out to her, but I was still so American, I did not know what to say—not to mention the fact that my Nyanja was not so good, and neither was her English. After greeting her, I made hand motions and spoke slowly saying that the party was over now. She said she was "chedwa miningi" (very late). I suggested that maybe she would like to come earlier for next month's tea. She, in turn, begged me to let her in. I did not have the heart to refuse her, but—for mercy's sake—this late thing was just carried too far! It was downright annoying in MY culture. Rats! I wished I could forget my culture, but it was almost impossible—like trying to drain the blood out of my vascular system. If I lost it, I would no longer be who I am!

I had a private struggle with myself and opened the gate. She came in—just like the others—apologizing for being a bit late. I now had no more cake or hot tea left. I asked Banda to find something in the kitchen to feed her while I bid the others goodbye. I heard the women tease as they passed her in the kitchen, "Latecomers eat bones" (an old, African proverb: the meat has been eaten).

I thank God for the Holy Spirit in times like this. I know it was He who restrained my irritated instincts and helped me to see an opportunity to fish. I was very tired, and personally longed for private space to "get over" my annoyance with these cultural differences. But here sat a late fish in my pond! We had to accept late just like I had to accept sick fish and different and needy fish. Again, it was I who changed, who became something I indeed was not. In doing so, this woman became my true friend from that point on. Her husband never allowed her to come to church, but he never refused her to attend my tea parties. There, she gave me her ears and her heart, as did several others. There, I gave them the wonderful gospel of Jesus Christ.

One of the other women who attended my parties often was a

rather refined, well educated woman, Mrs. M. She was not resistant to religion; merely stubbornly indifferent to salvation through Christ's death and His grace. She had a hard-core mentality that she was good, that her efforts to earn salvation were earnest and sufficient—at least in her mind. Whenever I came to the Bible study part of our tea party, she would put her head down, refusing to give eye contact until the devotional was over. Then—and only then—would she raise her eyes and resume connectedness. It was so obvious, that it was rude and annoying. She was certainly polite on the social level, but spiritual defensiveness made her about as easy to connect with as a piranha!

I was sincere in my concern for her welfare, and I wanted to give her a reason to consider the person of Christ. I spent a good deal of time thinking about her. I prayed about it. One day, the Lord brought to my mind a similar situation that my dad had shared with me years previously. He used to have a neighbor who was very closed and private. God brought to his attention the story of the woman at the well. Jesus' approach to opening her up was to show her His own need—in His case, for water. Dad asked his neighbor to keep his house key when they would travel. It opened up the relationship and developed a trust between them. I began to think about needs I had. I needed to learn to cook Zambian. Maybe Mrs. M. would teach me.

The next Tuesday, I paid a visit to Mrs. M. She treated me with the same caution as usual. This time, however, she brightened when I explained that I had a need. I had no experience cooking the foods they loved the best, and I wanted to learn. Would she be willing to help me? I offered to pay for any of the ingredients we might need, and she quickly agreed to get involved. Now that she was all eager, I got nervous.

"Well, let me give you the money, Mrs. M., and you can come to my house next Tuesday. We'll spend the morning cooking, and then feast together for lunch." I paused. She noted my hesitancy. I took a deep breath. "Mrs. M.? I hope you understand that I am somewhat new to Zambia, and I am not used to some of the foods that you have. So, if you could please be easy on me, I would be very thankful.

To begin with, I just need to say that I don't eat anything that is looking at me. So, if you would please not buy anything that has eyeballs, I would appreciate it." That eliminated the fried rats, caterpillar and insect dishes, that just did not hold my appetite's interest. A beautiful smile lit up Mrs. M.'s face. She promised to stick with plants, and to avoid eyeballs, and be at the house on Tuesday morning. I thanked her with relief.

Tuesday morning, Mrs. M. and another woman arrived early, shopping sacks and baskets in hand. I was prepared with my pots, cutlery, and note cards for taking down the recipes. I quickly learned that Zambian cuisine was anything but precise. It was all instinctive cooking—no recipes, no standard measurements, nothing written down, just pure hand-me-down traditions.

That morning I watched and wrote descriptions of what we were preparing: fwaka-fwaka, chiwawa with groundnuts, delele, impwe, and more. We prepared seven sauces, called relishes, which accompanied the nshima, a thick cornmeal mush served in "lumps." It was fascinating and time consuming. We pulled strings out of pumpkin leaves, chopped unidentified leaves (to me), onions, tomatoes, and vegetables. I was having a ball. Mrs. M. was as free and at home in my kitchen as if she lived there, no reservations. The conversation flowed freely as well.

At noon we were ready. I called the kids and Jim to the table. As I looked over the bowls before me, my stomach did a funny flip. I knew what was in each one, and had even helped to prepare them. However, they didn't look so good. If presentation is seventy percent of appetite, I could only hope that the thirty percent flavor had some appeal. This looked like recycled…something. While Jim was giving thanks for the food, I asked God to help me swallow it. I am not a picky eater, so I wondered if my stomach jitters were due to nerves and the anticipation that this fisherman might not be able to eat her own bait. There seemed to be so much at stake. I had to like it! I wanted to like it.

We raised our heads from prayer and began to pass the dishes, beginning with the nshima. I knew I liked that, already. I put a little of everything on my plate, as did each of the children. Most of it was really delicious, until I came to the delele (boiled okra). There is not a pleasant way to describe green chunks floating in a slimy solution, and there is not a pleasant way to swallow it, either. The consistency was something that only seemed to excite my gag reflex—to this day. I looked around at the kids to see how they were doing. One was trying to make the delele stay on the nshima, obviously ineffectively. Another was trying to transfer it from the dish to the plate, in one, long, stringy effort. I put my head down to hide a smile. I admitted defeat to that dish, and made the most of all the other relishes.

Mrs. M. was watching the family. There was no place for hypocrisy here. "How do you like it?" She queried.

The children stopped eating long enough to affirm their acceptance. I majored in raving about everything I really loved, and then added, "Umm, how do you eat that delele? I can't seem to catch it long enough to swallow it." She smiled and then laughed, showing me how expertly she could swab up the puddle on her own plate. Well, I was impressed. But it did not improve the swallowing action. Mine just recycled at the throat until I gave up and stopped embarrassing myself. The point was not whether I liked *every* dish, but whether I was willing to become Zambian in my ways. Even Zambians do not love *every* entrée served in the country.

I have since broadened my palate to some "eyeball" foods, and some consistencies formerly in the "unthinkable" category. It just took time and familiarity and a little persuasiveness to get beyond myself. The children have done better than Jim and I. They have tried rats and bugs and caterpillars with an ease that spurs us to attempt all things for all men. Bite for bite, we were learning the grace of eating and drinking for God's glory and honor, rather than pleasing ourselves. In doing so, I believe we also learned the joy of winning the trust and acceptance of many. I also thank God with unrestrained joy for the privilege of "fishing in the kitchen."

If I had to eat eyeballs or slime, I would do it to win ONE to Christ. As for Mrs. M., she died before she ever partook of Christ. It appears that she had no appetite for the Living Bread Who could satisfy her soul. She would not even "taste Him," for if she had, she would have seen that the "Lord is good!"[4] I grieved her death deeply, for I had coaxed her to eat and to be satisfied. Yet, a starving woman died at a lavish table of divinely prepared food. What a tragedy!

* * *

"This is the bread which comes down from heaven...
If anyone eats of this bread, he will live forever;
and the bread that I shall give is My flesh,
which I shall give for the life of the world."[5]

Chapter 21

Shearer Joy

One of the great privileges in life is friends—real friends—the kind that comes alongside in any situation and participates in whatever your circumstances. This is particularly true in the ministry, and the need for genuine friends during cross-cultural ministry only intensifies. In the first years of adjustment, change is unrelenting and tiring to the soul. A constant, unwavering friendship can be the difference between the desire to quit and the courage to press on. We have such friends. How kind of our Father, during times of distress and fatigue, that He sends the sweetest sort of encouragement—a friend that sticks closer than a brother.

We were nearly halfway through our first term. There had been adventures, laughter, and exhilarating challenges, but there had also been shock and fears and sorrows and feelings of failure. Our emotional meters read like the pattern of the Swiss Alps—craggy peaks and low valleys. Sometimes I wondered if we would ever adjust to the "new normal." It was challenging to just keep perspective, to find light-heartedness and rest for our souls. It seemed like we were always on alert for the next problem, and when it came, there were few there on the field on whom we could unload our souls.

The month of May 1993 opened with some real heavies to bear. In the last days of April, the Zambian National Soccer team crashed into the Atlantic Ocean, two miles off the coast of Gabon. The entire "dream team" with coaches and staff perished, and with them, all the hope of a tiny nation's glory in the sports world. This team touted the best goalie in Africa and was expected to win the Africa Cup. National pride and attention on this team had been at an all-time high; conversely, the shock and trauma of the nation lay at an all-time low. Adding to the darkness was the unexplained cause of the crash. President Chiluba declared a week of mourning. Drums beat all night in our neighborhood, deterring sleep in our household.

Sunday, May 2nd, the bodies of the team arrived in the city. We stood with hundreds of thousands at The Great East Road to watch thirty-some caskets in procession to the national Independence Stadium. We were so far back from the road we could barely see the somber lineup, but the sound of mourning or the hush of respect was just as unforgettable. I watched the faces of the Zambians. My own grief was for those who were sorrowing.

Monday, all businesses and schools were closed for the funeral; the nation shut down so that all its citizens could participate—some by radio, some by television, and thousands first-hand at Independence Stadium. Our family gathered to watch over ZNBC. President Chiluba, a man of small stature and great of heart, gave a very moving speech, quoting much Scripture, breaking down in places to weep this loss of life. His First Lady also wept; and at different times, the agonies of relatives and friends in the stadium burst out. The president prayed, thanking God for being in control of all things, praying for the comfort of the nation and the families. His leadership called the nation to turn to God, to find comfort in His sovereignty and salvation. Our family had never seen any dignitary so open about his faith in Jesus Christ. It gave great spiritual dignity and direction to Zambia. The entire team was buried as national heroes on the banks of the stadium.

As a dark spirit of grief lingered over the nation, there were other shadows which fell over us. Some of our marriage-counseling sessions were rather grey in their outcomes. The sessions uncovered murky, cultural differences in the way one defines and practices the covenant of marriage. So many times we felt in the dark about what to do about it.

We were also groping for solid relationships in this new land of indirect communications. Here, in Zambia, politeness was more important than straightforwardness; the appearance of social harmony was more acceptable than tough love and truthfulness. Again, there were uncertainties of how to handle it. It surfaced daily in personal relationships as well as in business affairs. When the electricity, phone, or water services were inoperable, appeals for assistance were addressed with the same, cultural shadiness: "We will come soon." To an African mind, that was being polite and respectful; to an American mind, it was pure dishonesty and highly annoying.

But the Son is always shining, and God gave us a few, bright rays to lighten our hearts in dim times. First, we heard there was a piano for sale. A missionary family experiencing serious health issues had to return to the States and was selling out. (They had been on a waiting list for that mission's piano for *five years*, and had only owned it less than two months!) One hour after hearing the news, we were driving across the city to see an old upright, a missionary hand-me-down for generations. The soundboard was cracked, but it still played beautifully. The following week, we brought it home, totally thrilled with such a precious and rare gift from God. My faith and prayers had been answered by a very trustworthy and compassionate Father. And the price was a fair agreement between brothers in Christ. I was dancing in my heart because God had promised and performed: "Ask and it shall be given unto you."[1] The children were eyewitnesses that nothing was impossible with God: water from a rock or a piano from within Zambia! There was music again in our hearts and home.

A second ray of pure Sonlight was word that dear family friends, the Shearers, were bringing a college puppet team to share in the ministry with us. The anticipation of their presence just about put our family through the roof with excitement. These people represented authenticity and faithful friendship. Letters went home: "I'm trying to get curtains sewed and hung in 'tweener times.' If I don't finish, I'll just sit down with Shearers and visit next to naked windows. I am determined to squeeze all the good fellowship juice they've got." Oh, how we missed these trustworthy friends! Jim wrote, "We are sure looking forward to seeing them again. We have learned nearly everything that we apply in ministry from Pastor Shearer, and our time under his leadership. It will be a privilege to hear his impressions of what he sees happening here."

While we anticipated Shearer joy, we were making more and more observations about the personal needs our family had for dependable friends. Relationships had a different purpose in this culture, they were meant to benefit an individual or family financially, materially, or socially. In our culture, we were used to people liking us for who we were, for the intrinsic value of the relationship itself. Here in Zambia, we often felt "used" for someone else's gain.

The kids' needs were a growing concern to Jim and me. Each one had different symptoms of some social deprivation and the stress of being used. Micah had been a boy of freewill generosity, but when his peers took from him, his young heart closed up protectively. He was too frequently asking, "How many more days 'til we go back to America?" Anne was cautious with her friendships, she did not like to commit until she recognized faithfulness and a return for her efforts. It was too soon for that. She turned to her bookworm preferences. Mary reached out liberally to others, but sometimes became frustrated with the language limitations or rough responses of the children: hair pulling, grabbing toys, and skin-pinching. Some of the children liked to "test" her color to see if the white skin and blonde hair were permanent and authentic. Harrison and Megan's friendship remained solid; he was her link to others, but not all our children had this "in" with Zambian circles. Nathan was outgoing and fun loving, but had not yet found someone with whom he could solidly relate. Many Zambians wanted his friendship, but again, for their own benefit. It was not satisfying at this stage of our relationships.

One young man exemplified this cultural expectation so well. He introduced himself to Nathan, and upon learning that he was an American (stereotype of being rich, white, and the key to status) said,

"Oh, my friend! You are my BEST friend." This was a startling statement, given OUR definition of a "best friend!" He then tried to make inroads into the relationship with Nathan. Not sure where to start, he opened with "So! Uh…how's MacGyver?" When Nathan explained that he was probably fine but that he did not know the man personally, the young man tried again. "So…how's the A-Team?" Nathan offered a kind explanation about his Mr. T's non-relationship, but—as expected —the friendship lacked much meaning. Such were some of our first associations with "friends."

Into this context, the Shearers re-entered our lives. They arrived on a memorable day, ours and the Bells' wedding anniversary, June 18th. The plane was an awful hour late, but it only increased our anticipation and the thrill of at last laying our eyes on them. There was Suzy, Micah's little friend; and Joni, who was Nathan and Anne's age; and Byron and Libby, our friends, advisors, and lovers of our souls. All visitors were happily welcomed, but our heart focus was riveted onto the Shearers when that plane landed. We stood on the observation deck, straining to catch a glimpse of them. It wasn't hard to pick them out, all dressed in yellow shirts. Jim whistled a shrill signal, and Byron caught sight of us, responding with a happy, windmill wave. They were a piece of home coming to us.

It was a great welcoming party and spectacle—missionaries and kids meeting each other. Stacks of luggage and trunks were crammed into any available, missionary vehicle along with bodies and backpacks. We headed to the Fogles' for a light brunch, prepared by Doreen. The fresh food, fresh adrenaline, and sweet hubbub in the place carried the travelers through initial jet lag…but not for long. Byron took the puppet team aside for last minute instructions, and they were dispersed into host homes with the missionaries. Shearers went with us, of course, bringing a daunting pile of luggage not their own; puppets, stage, and trappings; next year's school books and supplies; goodies and pleasure reading, and wonderful mail from home. Nathan took the lead in offloading into the grass courtyard inside our ex-mansion. He wrote,

"When all that was done, we unpacked those trunks. That was the most depressing time I've had since after mid-terms! Two WHOLE trunks were full of *our* school books. I don't think I will live past next year!"

By late afternoon, we had the Shearers all to ourselves. Mary and Micah shared Suzy who was Micah's age, and the three eldest went for a five-mile walk with Joni, working the kinks out, I guess. There was a feeling that we could just be ourselves. I wrote, "They are just like family: no pretenses or images to live up to. I can be myself, feel comfortable in my own place, and they still love me! Amazing!" We celebrated our reunion with good food, but savored real conversation that night like old and sweet times. "It takes a long time to grow an old friend."

The puppet team had been well-trained by Byron and Libby. They came prepared for large-group game activities, gospel messages through puppetry, music, and a story time. The very next day, they renounced fatigue and began ministry in Chawama. One hundred seventy five children turned up the first day. It was obvious that puppetry was a natural draw in this setting, more than we had anticipated. Libby said the children were packed so tightly together on the floor that no one

Shearers and the Cedarville Puppet Team

could step between them. A tiny path was left in the middle so that one could navigate from the front of the church shelter to the back. Group games had a new definition, an overwhelming definition for the college leaders. The attendance reached over four hundred by the last day, and the team was already bushed from so many blessings!

With only a few days to recover, the puppeteers moved to the Chelstone community. Again, attendance mushroomed as it had in Chawama. We were becoming nervous about where to host the team in our Chilenge neighborhood. There was no yard large enough for those kinds of responses. Even though our yard was large, it was not located in the actual community of the church, and the empty plot which the mission owned had no facilities whatsoever. God was good. To our pleasure and His glory, we rented the town hall, strategically in the center of the community, for ten dollars. Banda was more excited than any other person in the church. He posted fliers on trees and telephone poles in the neighborhoods, talking excitedly about the "Muppet Team" that had come from the United States.

Children responded in droves the first day. Then a teacher strike over pay issues closed the elementary schools, opening more opportunities for children to participate in the program. By the last day, the attendance was outrageous: we maxed over eight hundred! The challenge was what to do! Forty two made personal responses for counseling or inquiries about their salvation and spiritual needs. One of these was Christopher, a young, troubled teen. As an orphan, he struggled to find work and provisions for the relatives who had taken him in. He tried to drink away his thoughts, and now was in a vicious cycle of sin, alcoholism, depression, and bad friendships. He came with real earnestness to the Savior, looking for freedom. I asked him what it was that drew him to the town hall that day. His reply was memorable, "The Lord gave me a desire *for Him*!"

The next to the last day, Christopher heard the story of the prodigal son and of the father that loved and accepted him. He, too, confessed his wayward path from God, put his trust in Christ, and followed up with discipleship lessons and church attendance for years after. This did not lift his problems from his shoulders. He struggled after his profession to learn to walk in his new life, but the church began a ministry to him that continued for years to come.

The team's sacrificial service brought more than decisions. The long-term effects are better measured by God, but from our vantage point, we saw how their ministry raised the visibility of the church and built bridges into the community in the months that followed. When we walked the streets for visitation, people associated us with "that team from the United States." Trisha, one of the puppeteers, remained behind for a short internship with us. Her humility and sensibility was respected by the Zambians and added to the team's outreach, good association, and reputation for the church.

The puppet ministry took mornings, but the Shearer family was serving alongside us in multiple ways all day long. Byron preached in all three churches, taught a module in the Bible Institute, and connected into relationships with people in our congregation. Libby served everyone, and then served some more whenever she saw a need. We went for long walks so we could just talk about whatever our hearts wanted to expose. The Shearers were themselves going through transitions, determining next steps in their journey with God and ministry. We could mutually bear burdens and share joys. Mary, Suzy, and Micah squeezed every ounce of fun from every single day and every single person, celebrating everything from Suzy's birthday to Mary and Suzy's Olympic diving contests from the toilet to the bathtub, or mud-pie baking contests in the yard. Their laughter was a contagious melody around the house. Nathan, Joni, Anne, Megan and Harrison worked and laughed and linked together naturally. It was just good all the way around. As effective and zealous as Shearers were in ministry, their impact was not measured by their busyness, but by their relationships.

Probably one of the greatest benefits of a visit from friends was that they were able to experience our new life with us. It was amusing to watch their own adjustments to the differences. Some they took so graciously that they were an example for us. Others reminded us of our own jerky reactions to the change and culture of Africa. One Sunday, Byron was preaching in our house church. The message on "Blind Bart" kept the people's rapt attention, except for the babies. One child on the front row was particularly fussy, so the mother—as is normal for a Zambian—quieted her child with her breast. Poor Byron lost concentration, and we lost composure watching him grope for Blind Bart[imaeus] and a train of thought. The little culture shocks could catch even the best unawares!

Another fun experience was listening to them describe their new nighttime drills. Before they could turn the lights out, there had to be a routine cleansing of the room. All flying, biting, buzzing, or scuttering creepy-crawlies were expected to be two dimensional: FLAT! Once Byron and Libby were convinced the room was not "bugged," they could rest. One night, they had completed the "chambers' purge" when our thief alarm sounded, an ear-splitting siren. I hadn't mentioned a "fire drill" to this point. Alex appeared at our window breathless, reporting that "thieves had jumped the wall fence." He thought one had even climbed on the roof to enter our interior courtyard. Having no weapons of consequence on the property, we all gathered outside in the courtyard, looking at each other in our nightclothes and vulnerability. Alex was armed with a mere slingshot, and we, with nothing more threatening than barking dogs, a broom, plunger, and Libby's certification for self-defense. It was almost comical to think of us protecting ourselves against armed robbers. We whispered to each other and prayed for protection in the cold, night air. After nothing of consequence occurred, Jim called Alex out of hiding, and asked him to turn off the alarm. We returned to our rooms, shivering with chill and adrenaline. I forgot to ask if they had to re-cleanse the quarters before clobbering the sandman for the night.

The value of friends who step into your world on the mission field cannot be measured. Shearers understood us, weaknesses and strengths, and walked through our challenges with compassion and counsel. One Sunday while they were there, we were hosting our weekly youth meeting for the MKs. Jim was interrupted from his lesson by a man at the gate. It was a shocking notification that we were to be evicted from the premises. We had no clue as to the cause, but the notice informed us that we had three months to vacate the property unless we wanted to come up with funds to pay the "new" rent: $1,500/month. The next Tuesday, while Shearers were ministering with the puppets, we were handed a second notice: our electricity would be shut off on Wednesday if we did not pay back payments from the former tenant. Jim had to run in circles to get us cleared from that. After settling that issue, discussions began with the leasing party for the house. It was a very unjust situation, and we said so. The representative's comment was, "That is correct." I began to dread another move; it just did not make sense. How timely that God brought Shearer encouragement. Often, true friendship is just another way to spell perseverance.

I wasn't sure how I'd feel about their departure when the time came. The kids cried, and I got wet eyes when they waved their last goodbye from the top of the airplane steps. The benefits of their presence and exemplary ministry had impacted and encouraged more than ourselves. They would be missed by our church people, too. I was tempted to cling to them, yet I was filled with an unexplainable contentment. I was completely satisfied with their visit—satisfied enough to stay here for now. Even when we drove to the empty house, I felt like we were driving HOME, to our place, and I did not long to be somewhere else for "home."

* * *

*"A friend loves at all times, and a brother is born for adversity.
… there is a friend who sticks closer than a brother."*[8]

Chapter 22

School Daze

The calendar said it was time for school to begin, but the heat was enough to melt any zeal for that. The children began their classes August 23rd at the Fogle's new house just blocks from our home. Again, Larry and Jim refurbished a small building on the property for a classroom, and Sherry joined Sallie as "professors at the dining room table" until the schoolhouse was ready. Fall, regardless of the weather, was again going to be an intense time of learning for all, only this year, we had advanced one grade.

God seemed to choose the fall season in our lives for enrolling us in His own school of hard knocks, new lessons, and tests. He was constantly drilling us on our faith and then recycling that knowledge with cumulative exams. Another student (James, to be exact) warned us ahead of time to count the tests as joyful experiences—not because we are so astute; not because we are so comfortable and self assured— but because the testing times exercised endurance, a trait that would eventually enable us to complete the course. OK! We were enrolled!

The first two weeks of August were emotionally blah after the Shearers and the puppet team left. We had not taken a ministry break since our post-Christmas getaway to Kafue. Our little army of eight was a bit footsore from so much "marching in the army of the Lord." One lesson we were learning was the need "to come aside, and rest awhile." Jim booked a short, family getaway at "The Most High Hotel," a Christian managed oasis at Kariba, Zimbabwe where we could kick off our shoes for a recess. The timing was perfect. Upon our return, the dollar began a plunge that would seriously restrict our resources for months.

As we all entered school, the congregation—now too large for Mr. Mutantika's yard or our house—also entered the classrooms at Chilenge Basic School. The school was centrally located, increasing our visibility and accessibility in the community's eyes. As a church, we were happily growing in spiritual knowledge, numbers, and friendships. The three oldest children teamed up with Sherry to develop the children and youth ministry. Jim and I focused on the adults, watching God draw people to Himself and the church in steady growth: some came through visitation, some from the puppet outreach, some from good teaching, some through budding relationships. The soccer outreach was one of these.

Jim and Nathan had been passing the Woodlands stadium each week, keeping an eye on a group of hard-playing guys in the stony ground next to the stadium. Knowing Nathan's desire for competitive sports, Jim stopped to ask if they would let him join their game. The guys looked him over hesitantly. Nathan sized up the field with just as much reservation: there were broken beer bottles, stones, and a flat, worn-out ball for bare feet. The challenge was: how in the world do you guys play in these conditions?

Jim broke the awkward moment with some incentive: he would bring a good ball and pump, and even referee the games if they would let Nathan play. The guys brightened. By the next week, all the details for a new outreach were in place. Forty-five showed for the first game! (A little crowded, but definitely memorable!) The second week, thirty-five came. Banda was also recruited as a left-wing striker. He was quick on his feet, could score from the left, and impress even the best with his killer, over-the-head back kick. At the games, relationships and trust began to develop. Jim invited the guys to church and made himself available to talk over concerns or spiritual issues. Nathan connected with those who were willing to associate with him. This is how Sam and Nathan became best friends, and Sam was introduced to Jesus Christ. Sam later became a professional soccer player for Zambia.

Not every lesson at church was so much fun to teach or so easy to learn. Jim was facing some brick-wall thinking on how and who should build the church's facility. The assumption was that the missionary had all the money; the missionary was the spiritual parent; therefore, the missionary should build the house for his spiritual children. It sounded so obvious to their way of thinking, yet God was presenting a test of mind: reconsider what church stewardship required of them. It was a test of faith each Sunday, when the poverty of each member made offerings meager. Some wanted to raise revenues for a building fund by starting a nursery or preschool program. Some suggested we women make and sell crafts as fundraisers. No one suggested that tithes and offerings would ever suffice for constructing a building.

Jim was concerned that we follow a Biblical precedent. After teaching and preaching this for several weeks, he felt like we were back to first grade. The mindset was heavily set for us to finance everything including paying their labor! Jim was tested for strength and comprehension on this point. The Biblical precedents confronted the church to do something! Several donated time for making cement blocks, and some donated food for the workers. Offerings and our own limited resources began to purchase cement and building materials. Nothing happened quickly, but small progress was being made as we worked through this lesson together.

God's exams can be hard. As the Master Teacher passes them out He says "endure hardness."[1] A series of personal difficulties hit us that fall in rapid fire. We still had not resolved the housing eviction notice, but I thought that the Master Teacher was just testing us on trust. I didn't think we would really have to move, because we were using the house for God's glory and He was blessing that. Secretly, I expected God to come at the last minute with a big flourish, rescue us with His mighty hand, and maybe even bring some kind of vengeance on that greedy and unreasonable landlady, just like in the movies. At least, that was MY plan for Him. Whatever happened to that lesson I'd learned years ago: "My thoughts are not your thoughts...."[2]

Jim began searching for affordable housing. The prices were ludicrous, and the drop in the dollar and in financial giving from the States made our already thin budget a "none-of-the-above" answer. A three-bedroom house was asking $4000 per month, and an apartment was over $1,000. We continued to ask and search, hoping that our eviction notice was just a test, and only a test, of faith.

Our finances were stressing us out. We were down to the essentials; the money for fun or treats just was not available. I struggled at team meetings when others had the ability to go together for bulk orders of cheese or meats, and we did not. This was a test of character. We were very limited, and it was getting tighter. We majored on vegetables, beans and rice, lentils and rice, nshima and relishes, oatmeal, bread, eggs, and fresh fruits. While it was perfectly healthy, it was a test of my contentment. I felt the internal strain come and go.

Then there was a test of patience. We had been five weeks without daily water service. The city was on electricity and water rations. I wrote my parents, "I'm not real excited to face another day without water. It's so depressing not being able to flush toilets, bathe, wash the dishes or do laundry! It's bad. For the last three weeks, we have only had water ONE hour a day (from 5:00–6:00 a.m.) We try to fill the water tank... but there is not enough water pressure to force it up..." To a friend I added, "My whites no longer exist. We had to recycle water so much that they are seriously dingy grey. We hauled water in buckets some, but haven't had hot water for too long. There is not enough water pressure to get it into the hot water tanks." The prolonged limitations of water, electricity, and essentials tested me sorely. I began to gravitate towards thoughts of comforts from home and family. I wrote: "[when] we lack many necessities like water, it is an emotional frustration. But when we lack time with the ones we love, separated from their presence and comfort, it is a hardship."

163

God did not let up. He added more. Becca pulled a door over onto her, knocking out her two, freshly cut teeth. Then she contracted another case of dysentery, followed by a serious bout of thrush, and then spiking fevers. This time it was malaria. Heavy duty flu bugs hit the family next. Somewhere in that setting, Megan picked up a case of lice from carrying around some sweet, African babies. Being a large family, we each had our turn with lice, just as we'd had to share the experience of skin worms. Jim wrote a friend, "It has been very helpful for me to focus on God and not on the trials. Besides that, it helps me to be able to help the Africans; they face trials too." A personal test for me was next.

One Sunday night, Nathan wanted a warm bath. He asked if he could use the pressure cooker to heat the water, and I said yes, if he knew how to use it. I was standing next to the stove peeling vegetables, when he tried to force the lid open. Before I could get any words of warning out, the lid blew off! I screamed in pain and shock as the water and steam scalded my arm, torso and thigh. I was actually in shock, not able to sort through anger at the unwanted pain. Nathan was in a daze himself. He had been able to jump backwards, but I was sandwiched between the stove and counter.

Jim ran into the kitchen when he heard my screams. He shouted at me to run to the bathtub at the back of the house. I was too thick-headed. I protested that the waste water in the tub would cause infection, but there was no other option. Not one drop of clean water could be squeezed from any faucet in the house. Again, he shouted for me to get into the dirty, cold water, trying to reason for me. I was afraid and shuddering out of control. Jim forced me into the freezing waste water. Large sheets of skin came off as we removed my outer clothing. The sight of it only increased my violent quaking and teeth chattering.

Jim ran for the phone, praying it would work. He called the Fogles. Sallie was an RN, and of course, dearer and nearer to us than any other human resource. She spent the first few hours nursing me through the shock and pain. It was not wise for us to find medical help at that hour of the night, as no clinic that we trusted was open and there was a curfew in place due to a political threat. Sallie was comforting and wise, giving me something for pain until we could get to our American doctor the next morning. Hers and Larry's sweet friendship walked through our trauma and the healing process with us, helping with the family needs until I could manage better. These were lessons of grace through friendship, and the Fogles earned an A+. "Though he causes grief, yet will He will show compassion."[3]

The housing situation continued to try our hearts. We were to be out by the end of October, and I was slow to pack up. I had imagined and convinced myself that God would not let his children face such an injustice without intervening. But it did not seem like He was coming through on my plan. I just didn't get this!

I wrote a key entry in my journal:

*A certain man said to Jesus, "Lord, I will follow You wherever You go." Jesus said, "Foxes have holes, and birds … have nests, but the Son of Man has no where to lay his head."[4] I had never really identified with that feeling before now. I've changed houses four times in less than a year and a half, and now, with five days before moving, we still have nowhere to lay our heads in a residence of our own. Maybe we were not being tested on "justice." Maybe this test was over something else: "Take my yoke upon you, and **learn of ME**."[5] Something of this scenario resembled in a minute way, what the Lord Jesus experienced when He came into "our neighborhood."*

By my birthday, October 26th, the house was barren looking, all packed up with no place to go. Our furniture was distributed to the homes of other missionaries until we could relocate. My feelings were too wobbly, and the wallet was too thin for celebrating with a flare. We were on our last ten dollars before the next remittance and still had to buy groceries. My birthday present from Jim was meat for our supper. The kids fixed special treats from supplies we already had and gave me a tablecloth they'd purchased in August. I wrote a close friend: "I had my birthday; I got one present; I got older."

The question surfacing during this time was "why?" Why would God let us suffer like this: burns, sickness, financial stress, injustice, eviction? What were His learning objectives for these tests? The answers were not to be revealed immediately. We only knew we were not to lean on our own understanding of the situation. I battled with disillusionment. I did not feel pious about the problems. I felt bewildered by them. But this was all part of gaining experience. Didn't Paul say something about that somewhere? "…we glory in tribulations also, knowing that tribulation works patience, and patience [works] experience [a testedness]."[6] Later, much later, I found a comment from Oswald Chambers which described my "schooling experiences" that fall:

"The servant of God has to go through the experience of things before he is allowed to go through the study of them. When you have had the experience, God will give you the line for study; the experience first, and then the explanation of the experience by the Spirit of God. Each one of us is an isolated person with God, and *He will put us through experiences that are not meant for us at all, but meant to make us fit stuff to feed others.*"[7]

We located a newly constructed house in a developing neighborhood about fifteen minutes from the church. The rent for this tiny, three-bedroom home was negotiated to within $100 of what we could afford, but we were required to pay the entire six-months rent in advance. We borrowed from our passage-home account to pay the huge lump sum. A personal supporter, sensitive to our financial crisis, offered to cover the extra $100 per month so that we could finish out our term. It was all a step of faith and a provision of God, not what I'd expected, just what we needed. We cut down, cut back, and cut out everything we knew in order to finish our course. I must have been learning something during these times. An amazing journal entry around the end of October read:

Up at five rejoicing…just thinking how the worst of weeks has turned into the joy of joys. The Lord has been gracious in abundant ways. Oh, that I would walk in His Spirit like this all the time!

Though we are living frugally by earthly resources, I'm full and satisfied in the blessing and presence of my dear Lord. How can I thank Him enough!

The new house was not going to be ready for occupancy for weeks. Sherry offered her own place until we could move in, and Doreen opened her home for Sherry. We now had "a plan," and a reason to relax from the tension of uncertainty. Larry and Sallie, knowing intimately of our struggles, gave us the gift of a night away, staying with our children so that Jim and I could have some personal time to regroup before the move. Friends like these were better than money or comfort or a smooth life.

The lessons from these days are still being used in my life today. We were taught, and we were tested so that we could be approved to encourage others. I was learning by scrape and by scar that God is dependable, regardless of disillusionment or disappointments from our faulty understanding. I was also experiencing the value of teammates who were first and foremost friends. I look back over my shoulder with an affectionate eye upon their loving sacrifices. I wrote a dear friend, "…in eternity, we might take the time to realize how much we influence and need one another."

● ● ●

"Blessed be God…the God of all comfort; Who comforts us in all our tribulation, that we may be able to comfort those who are in any trouble, with the comfort with which we ourselves are comforted."[8]

Chapter 23

Celebrations

October 31ˢᵗ was moving day. I continued to look at my watch, off and on throughout the day. I was giving time for God to send someone to the gate at this last opportunity, renouncing this eviction or sending an apology. I felt slightly agitated that the Lord was not rescuing us from this injustice, but I still believed He would come through. That is why I kept looking at my watch. Jim had clearly given up that idea. It is a good thing I married a realist, and that God gave me six, hard-working children! We finished mopping the floors and hauling boxes out to the van by dusk. By supper, we were at Sherry's place. Doreen had prepared a supper for us, and I was more than grateful. Simple food and a place to lie down felt like reasons to celebrate. I was ashamed of my feelings earlier in the day, but struggled in my heart with confusion and disillusionment.

The next three weeks of being displaced were utterly packed with activity. Prior to our move, I had taken on several writing and directing projects for upcoming holiday festivities. One of these was for the American Embassy's Thanksgiving service. The children from the American International School were to perform, and this was to be televised on ZNBC. We were also asked to sing as a family for the program. At the time, I thought I must have been nuts to accept the responsibility; I already had too much to do, and I was still trying to find essentials in our scattered belongings. However, the focus on

Thanksgiving practices was a perfect diversion from the other realities we were living.

We had a few incidents to address, at our temporary abode. Our first discovery was that the dogs were a strain on every good grace and intention in our relationships. Copper, our new puppy, crawled under Tin Lizzy to chew apart the wires. It took Jim and another missionary an entire morning to reattach the electrical system, and much longer to reconnect with the dog in a friendly manner. Then, we all made a brilliant discovery: our dogs and Sherry's dogs were territorial males! The daily tension between the dogs put everyone on edge, culminating with a Friday night incident. Sherry left the guard house door ajar, and Okey tore into Sherry's dog, "Bear." Not only did we have to make several trips to the veterinary, but it took some grace to repair feelings of owners, too.

We might have "patched" up quickly had we not been aggravated by our own human bloopers. Sherry had been so gracious to give us her very best. Her package deal included her own queen-size water bed, a euphoric improvement from Anne and Megan's foam, twin mattresses. They slept in "fairyland"…until…Megan's new, handmade comforter was used as the "icing on the cake." There were still pins in her sewing project! The bed wet on the girls, and its bladder took a greater part of the day to drain and repair! Sherry was perturbed; Jim was even more so; and the girls were abruptly demoted from fairyland to foam. Being human instead of fairies or celestial flyers (alias, angels) seemed to be our specialty.

One incredible break came from God. The conductor of the Lusaka Music Society was leaving the country with his wife, who was Megan's piano teacher, for a week-long break. They asked if our family would be willing to house sit for them. Their beautiful home had a pool, conveniences, music, food, and lovely gardens. We accepted, relieved to be pulled out of the boxes and stacks of our temporary dwelling. The children swam, played the two pianos, the harpsichord, watched videos, and slept in delightful beds. The getaway, completely free of charge, provided time to refresh ourselves—another celebration of Thanksgiving.

The Sunday before the holiday was the American program at the Ambassador's home. The school students performed perfectly; and our family sang two Scripture songs and quoted a choral reading of Psalm 67. Some in the audience may have felt awkward, but God did not. He was honored. Afterwards, I roamed through the Ambassador's open home, taking in the lovely china, furnishings, and wall décor. Many commented on the drama and songs, but two women particularly drew me in. The Ambassador's wife shared kind words of gratitude for our family singing together. Her friend, the wife of the auditor for the World Bank warmly took my hand as she related how we had ministered while she was missing her own family. I was humbled to think I could even minister at all.

We moved into the new house the week of Thanksgiving. The entire first floor could have fit into the living room of our old house, and the upstairs into our dining room. But, we were now home, hopefully for the last time until we returned to America. The boys, as opposite as messy and "cleanie," now shared a room. Anne and Megan shared the other, while Mary and Becca were put into the breakfast nook, which also served as the office and the playroom. The kitchen had three base cupboards and a small pantry, but no room for a table. I felt rather compact with our family of eight, definitely downsized in space and extras.

Thursday, we had a wonderful Thanksgiving with the team. After a fabulous meal with the Fogles we sang together and gave one-liner testimonies of God's work in our lives. A volleyball game and homemade pies made it fun and festive. When we left for home I was happier than I had been for weeks. The team spirit refreshed us and a lovely surprise awaited us in Tin Lizzy. She was stuffed with food supplies, a personal shower from the Bells.

I wrote:

I am regaining some perspective and praise in my life. I look back over the last month and say with enthusiasm that God has given me some of the richest blessings human life can offer: His mercy during my time of faltering faith, His Word to restore me, and the best Christian family and friends anyone could have. The team went out of their way to give us every kind of support and practical help imaginable during our transition. Letters and phone calls from the States reiterated the love that I needed to hear at this time.

The day following, we had the Viyolas for dinner. Jim had led Mr. Viyola to Christ last December. Now Mrs. Viyola had become open, challenging us with some real questions about faith, salvation, good works, and beliefs. This meal was a follow-up to address her inquiries and to share a video which specifically explained the Bible's answers to her questions. The time together was excellent. We determined not to press her for a decision, but to let her take whatever time she needed to study and respond to the truths we'd given her. We would soon be seeing a difference if she had received Christ. Two weeks later, we heard the good news that she had placed her trust in Christ for salvation! We exploded with joy!

Saturday was the usual visitation day. We stopped at one of our young widow's home. Here she lived with her two very ill sisters, both struggling for life because of tuberculosis. The one was so broken in spirit; the other, simply desperate to live. What a time and opportunity to speak of eternal life through the provision of Jesus Christ! The hunger and thirst to live was ravenous. One clung to our words and received the Truth of God meekly and gratefully. The other—politely. In this context, I felt the significance of celebrating the Incarnation year round, knowing the Lord Jesus was more than a Christmas babe. He was Life to dying people and acceptance with God for hopeless sinners. This was like Christmas and Thanksgiving every day.

As I walked down the dirt street to my next stop, I noted the idle teen girls flirting with the boys. I had a growing concern for them, too. Many were entering into physical promiscuity and eventual death while playing the roulette game with HIV and with sin. Some of these were the girls coming to our Bible class…and memorizing Scripture verses!

Some were professing that they had salvation, but they continued to follow their raw instincts naively. I loved them. I knew I needed to help them, but how and when?

Reaching the other end of the street I visited the home of one of the women from my ladies' teas. The woman had died the week before, but her daughter still attended our church. I entered the home where the elderly women of the clan greeted me in Nyanja. They were de-winging flying termites for lunch. I greeted them in return, and this caused them to think I knew Nyanja fluently. Much to my amazement I survived fifteen minutes of Nyanja conversation and managed to politely avoid suggestions of caterpillars, termites, and nshima for lunch. In the midst of my Christmas baking mentality, this was a small cause to celebrate! A big cause was that I comprehended and communicated in their language, without a translator's help!

The Christmas season brought many festive opportunities to lighten our hearts and bring others joy. Anne and I played in the Christmas concert for the Lusaka Music society. The next weekend our family sang together and produced a humorous skit for a large audience gathered at the Southern Baptist School, a prelude to a children's musical, "Getting' Ready for a Miracle." Some of our children were involved in the drama and songs. Three-year-old Mary played the part of a young angel. However, she discovered that this celestial vocation lacked activity so she yawned and dipped and gawked at whatever grabbed at her attention. She slipped her arms in and out of the sleeves making the empty fabric flap like wings, completely oblivious to the main drama of the stage while creating her own. If no one else noticed, it WAS the MIRACLE of the night. Her big brothers found more joy in her presentation than they could handle with composure. They had to leave for the restroom.

The Japanese embassy doctor, a neurosurgeon, and his wife were in the audience. After the program they invited our family to sing the following weekend at their personal Christmas. We sang a beautiful Polish carol and the lullaby to Jesus, "I Love You, Lord." The wife was so gracious, giving us generous gifts from Japan and introducing us to their guests. It was quite a connection for us.

Afterwards, we returned to our own happy reality. Everyone scattered into secret corners of the house to work on Christmas gifts for one another. Our scanty income was a lovely catalyst for creativity and gifts of love and time: wood projects from Nathan and Jim, sewing projects and crafts from the girls and me, homemade goodies from our kitchen. Simple and personal were the best gifts. This year's African Christmas was laid back and unpressurized. It gave us time to enjoy the gift of one another in unhurried leisure. There was even time enough to prepare for yet another performance on December 23rd, a carol-sing with new friends from Navigators International.

Christmas Eve was spent with the Fogles, exchanging gifts and drinking hot chocolate. Never mind that the weather was hot and humid, a steamy drink on Christmas Eve was "tradition," and it gave me the memory of a crisp, white Christmas past. Sharing the celebration with loved ones satisfied our need for togetherness and the felicity of old times at this season. Memories were good for reliving what could not be reproduced.

Christmas day opened with Becca standing at the edge of her Pack 'n Play hollering with arms outstretched, "MaaaMere! C'mere!" Once picked up, she gave her attention to Aunt Sherry who had joined us for a festive breakfast. We left for church, calm for once. I'll let Nathan tell his edited version of the program:

We arrived at our "reserved" room with plenty of time to spare. We remembered everything necessary, for once. We were actually prepared and did everything right, but what didn't go right was, for sure, not our fault! The keys to our "reserved room" were never given to the people we were supposed to get them from. (Can you believe it? I mean, come on here, folks!) When we finally got in, set up the seating and decorations, [wrapping paper, computer-made-banners, and ribbons-sticky tacked to the walls] we were only forty-five minutes late! The crowd wasn't big, but the ones who did come have been faithful. Everything down to the refreshments went like a breeze. Dad even kept his speaking to ten minutes! It was truly a miracle ordained from on high. After an hour, we dismissed and went home.

This was culture shock. Everything was so nearly predictable that it was beginning to feel like the wrong continent. We were even home for a big Christmas meal with the Fogles, Doreen, and Sherry by noon! What on earth! In the evening, we returned to the Fogles for hot chocolate and the newest version of Charles Dickens' "A Christmas Carol."

The grand finale of the day was our personal gift exchange. The time alone made me so grateful for all our financial scarcity. It brought out the best in our consideration and efforts for one another. Nathan's gifts were: a wooden rubber-band gun to Micah; carved bookends to Jim; and a unique spice rack to me. The girls surprised one another with their new sewing skills and crafts. Megan made a "girly" dress for Mary with a "twirly" skirt! Mary had to see if it puffed out when she spun around and she twisted her feet around one another until she landed hard on the floor. Though Jim did not twirl in the sport shirt I made him, I twirled in the delight that it looked like a shirt on him. My sewing efforts were just that—efforts! The joy of this exchange was in knowing how we had pleased one another.

The holidays this year had been such a personal gift from God. Though there was not much money, though we received no cards or letters or packages from home (there was a three-week postal strike), God chose to wrap these days in His own wealth: someone once said, "Measure wealth not by the things you have, but by the things you have for which you would not take money."

* * *

"I counsel you to buy from Me gold refined in the fire, that you may be rich, and white garments, that you may be clothed..."[1]

Chapter 24

I Will Build My Church

With the beginning of the New Year came a fresh urgency to strengthen the infant church at Chilenge before our June 1st furlough. Our new babes in Christ were wobbly in their progress, but growing and gaining health from the good milk of the Word. We wanted to pump as much spiritual nourishment into them as they could hold, and walk alongside them during these first exciting steps. On January 16th Jim baptized nine who were ready to walk in obedience to Christ. Among them were Harrison, Mrs. Viyola, and our own Micah. Jim wrote a personal account on February 21st that best describes his heart and experiences as a first-time pastor. The church's growth was a joy and fascination equal to that of raising a first-born child.

The church work, even though it takes a lot of time, has been a real blessing of late. We had nine baptized. It was a thrill to be part of the service—my first one! I was able to recount the growth of each individual as we were in the baptismal pool together at the Church of Christ who allowed us to use their facilities. It is still hard to imagine that I was the one who did the baptizing. I feel so unworthy to be called a pastor, but I count it a real privilege as well. God's working is magnificent! I think the greatest privilege of all was baptizing Micah. As his father, I never thought that I would be the one to baptize him; it was a real thrill for me!

We had some workdays at the church... a result of the desire to see the people do something that would make them realize they were an important part of the process. We challenged the people to do what they could, even if they did not have the money to buy materials. We wanted them to know that everything they give to God will be blessed as they give out of the principle of faithfulness. Rachel came up with the idea of the women making crafts to sell in the market— the proceeds going toward building materials. The men and boys have been making cement blocks. We made three hundred blocks so far, but we were "rain assisted." We had to redo several because the rain made them collapse. You ought to try and lift a wet concrete block along with its steel form. Takes a lot of stamina and grit to keep at it! A couple people have the ability to contribute money; they are doing so as well. This whole process has been neat.

We have also been seeing results from the soccer outreach ministry. One of the guys who comes every week was finally persuaded by Mr. Banda to come to church for the Christmas service. Sam had been on my heart for a long time. I called on him with the intention of seeing if he had any questions about God that I might be able to answer. I had given him a Bible the week before and had placed a tract inside on how to be saved. He didn't really have any questions, but when I asked if he knew he would go to heaven if he died that day, he said he didn't know. I asked him if he wanted to and he said yes. So I had the opportunity of sharing the Gospel with him; he responded by trusting Christ as his Savior. He seems to be genuine, because he has been encouraging the other guys who come and play soccer to come to church. We have had at least four of the football guys in services to hear the good news of salvation. After the game the next week, I never had the opportunity to invite the guys to church; Sam did it. When the guys laughed, he looked them straight in the eyes and said, "You NEED to be there!"

…Mrs. Banda has been coming to the services! She often would get up and leave the service to care for her baby; then she would not return. Lately, she remains, listening intently. Perhaps God will bring her to Himself. Oh, that would be GLORY for us! Mrs. Viyola

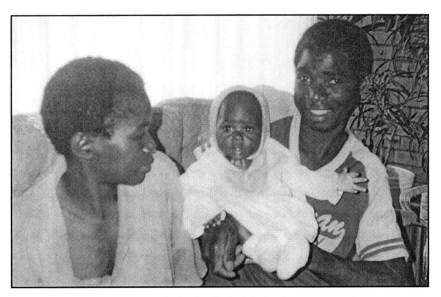

Mr. and Mrs. Banda with baby Grace

*surely has been an encouragement to us! It has been wonderful to see
her involved in every word that is spoken at church. She is the one
who is hosting the women's class and ladies' teas with Rachel.*

*As I close, I would just like to ask you to pray that we would keep
focused and be able to make good decisions over the next few months.
There is so much to distract our minds.*

There was a valid reason for making that prayer request. This was
our first experience at pioneering a church. We thought we were
responsible to do it all, plus more. Jim was pushing for the building to
be completed *by* the Zambian church, a task which took much longer
than if we had done it ourselves. Jim was hesitant to do more work
himself than would be wise for an example or for their participation.
He also stepped up the visitation, even though we were feeling the
time crunch from the new course we were writing and teaching at the
Bible Institute. We also chose to reinstate the weekly Bible studies and
activities for the missionary kids. Our children needed personal renewal,
attention, and fun. If we wanted that to happen, we pretty much had
to make it happen ourselves.

In the midst of a full plate, I could not shake my deep concern for our teen girls. I was so burdened for their safety and salvation. After seeing the devastating results of HIV, early deaths, and wasted lives, I felt responsible to do something before it was too late. "Hear a word from My mouth, and give them warning from me. When I say to the wicked, 'You shall surely die,' and you give him no warning… to save his life, that same wicked man shall die in his iniquity; but his blood I will require at your hand. Yet, if you warn the wicked, and he does not turn from his wickedness… he shall die in his iniquity; but you have delivered your soul."[1] The only thing I knew to deliver them, or me, was to teach God's plan of sexuality in contrast to traditions and fleshly instincts. The truth was: "There is a way that seems right to a man, but its end is the way of death."[2]

Alice Wimer, a veteran missionary, had taken six months to disciple me in a class that was developed for young girls in Chad. Using this as a base I adapted the curriculum for the girls; it lent itself to open questions, clear information and appropriate Biblical context. We talked about sexual intimacy from its beautiful intention to its raw abuse. I was frequently shocked at how little knowledge they had and at how much experience was available. The class was an incredible highlight in my life and gave direction to the girls. At last I was building a fence at the top of the cliff instead of a hospital at the bottom.

The process of growing a church included broadening the people's vision for others. Steve and Ruth Ann had the foresight to begin a village outreach in Lumbembe, about two hours south of Lusaka. They presented the opportunity to the mission team with the idea that this could develop a mission mindset for the churches and an evangelistic training experience for the Bible Institute students. It was a great idea—even if it was perhaps premature for the fledgling congregations to support. The three churches alternated responsibilities monthly. When it was our turn, the people were excited to be involved. We did not have anyone ready to teach or preach, so Jim preached through translators. This was our first "safari hat" experience in Africa.

The villagers sat on four-inch wide benches for as long as three hours at a time and listened with rapt attention to the teaching of the Word. Afterwards we shared the meal that we brought since the villagers were struggling for food because of a drought. At their own initiative our members shared their used clothing with the poor. These were the first steps of evangelization and compassion for our young congregation.

The way God built His church blew my mind some days. We were in the midst of a pandemic plague and economic struggle. Homes were filled with too many mouths to feed, neglected orphans, depressed caregivers, and sick loved ones. I found myself examining the Scriptures about what a healthy church was supposed to look like. From what I could gather these circumstances were closer to the Biblical models for growth than some of the sterilized situations I had observed in the United States. With so much death and sickness there was not going to be a booming attendance, but Christ truly manifested Himself brilliantly in such dark circumstances.

For example, we had two young sisters whom we visited weekly. Their tiny polished home was filled with caring family, but was marred by suffering from incurable diseases. Their thin frames marked their time and their sufferings. One day when I came to visit, I was bombarded by a pointed question: "Mrs. Chambers, Loveness said she got saved! What does that mean: she got 'saved'?" I explained what I had been gradually trying to tell her before, but never getting through. I explained the forgiveness of sins, the payment of Christ's lifeblood as the fee for our salvation; the need to accept that and trust what He did for us. She wanted this salvation. At last! She bowed before God right there on her bed and asked for God to forgive and to save her. What a radiant joy followed! Though she could barely sit up, she wanted to come to church, so each Sunday her healthy cousin, who also lived in the house, gently draped her over her own back. Her bony limbs dangled from her torso as her cousin walked her to our van and placed her on the seat.

The drive to church on the muddy potholed road was mercifully short. Once there, we removed the van seat so that she could endure sitting through the service. She had no muscle or fat to pad her. When suffering restricted her to the house she pursued her knowledge of Christ through a discipleship course we gave her. Megan, who loved crafts and handwork, helped her learn the new skill of cross stitch which gave her some sense of accomplishment from her bed. As the reality of Christ began to penetrate the home, the other sister also accepted the work of Christ for her salvation and later was baptized and joined the church. The sisters were too ill to share in the normal functions of the church, but they—like others—were part of the growth of our congregation until they left for heaven. In their absence, the Lord provided fruit for the seed of their faith; their mother and other family members, too, became an intrinsic part of the church through faith in Christ.

My human evaluations about the church's growth, i.e. counting attendance in my head, comparing it to last week's, or registering how many Bible studies or outreaches we were having, were inconsequential to the real progress that God was making. We were planting, yes, and loving the people; others were watering; but God was making the growth happen. It was all according to His own plan and intention to call out of misery, out of sickness, out of Zambia a people that would praise and love Him, people that would be His own. His compassion for the people—the teens, the soccer players, those dying, the orphans, the villagers—was drawing them to Himself, and one day He would gather them lovingly together in His arms, a mature bride, a grown-up church, beautiful and holy for Himself. We were just a small part of church growth, but a happy part.

* * *

"Faithful is he that calleth you, who also will do it."[3]

Chapter 25

The Other Missionaries

We were well into the last months of our first term. The children now had some experience in becoming missionaries. They'd lived with some hardships, some sicknesses and some "going without." Their personal sacrifices for God and their family could have been overlooked or simply assumed, but they were the ones who lived daily with God's summons. They absorbed the impact of family change and of a global transfer. They often bore heavy loads at home, felt the loneliness of being culturally out of place or struggled with scanty educational and social options in unfamiliar places. The longer we were there the more we realized that they could wither from being uprooted or grow strong from being transplanted. We prayed for the latter.

Either way, our kids were the "other missionaries." They had fully participated in nearly every ministry that we had. How Jim and I appreciated the willing attitude and vigor of our children for the work of God! Without their teamwork we would have been ineffective. God had done His work in their lives—as He had in ours—creating the desire to work for His own pleasure. Yea! That excited us! As parents we were not capable of producing six willing sacrifices, no matter if we drilled them with Bible verses or bribed them with benefits. This was a God thing, "that no flesh [parent] should glory in His presence."[1] The children were *God's* heritage and *His* reward. Jim and I were just grateful recipients of the teammates that energized us, kept us laughing and kept us sane when we were pressed beyond reason.

Megan carrying Mary and Becca in a chitenge

The children were the best bridge into the hearts of our Zambian community. However, being a bridge meant they were "walked on" at times. Initially the girls' blonde hair was yanked and their white skin was pinched by curious children. Anne and Megan were stared at and laughed at and poked at until their genuineness was proven to the Zambians. Nathan had to live with some prejudice on the soccer field until he had proven his sportsmanship, his teamwork, and his skill. It was to be expected: we were the foreigners! Our kids had to earn their own acceptance, and this was, again, not something we as parents could "arrange." This was a test of our children's own personal character and of God's enablement for them. It was also a test of our character and patience as parents. Parental instincts to protect and to control had to be balanced with the bigger picture of what God was teaching them.

Much of missionary life for kids or adults is relationships. When the kids invited children into the house some factors surfaced. First, our house was full of intriguing luxuries to an African mind, many of which lured the attention and desire of the Zambian children. It was not unusual to discover toys, toiletries, or possessions missing or broken after friends went home. We had to decide if we wanted friends or if we wanted belongings. In some cases we could have both, in others we chose which belongings could be shared and which should be kept out of sight for personal reasons. We had to learn to hold stuff loosely and people tightly. On the other hand, when friends had no care for the children, but only for their belongings, the relationship was a washout anyway. While the children had hearty dispositions, they also had limitations that needed respect. It was a delicate balance to find.

Family times were the best part and the hardest part of mission life. The only times we were actually alone as a family was after dark so suppertime was usually a celebration of being left to ourselves. It was fun. It was necessary. Mealtime was more than stuffing food into bodies; it was the emotional renewal and connectedness that nourished the soul. It was not uncommon for us to linger at the table for more than an hour each night, just talking about stuff or laughing over our discoveries. A family game of Boggle or Scattergories was not unusual nor was just hanging out in the same room until bath time—some with books, some with toys.

The three youngest usually provided our entertainment, whether they tried to or not. One meal, Mary was having a real struggle. She kept losing her balance while sitting on her knees and continually bumped my elbow as she tried to maintain control of herself and a tuna-egg sandwich. Her "sammich" innards kept falling onto the table. Mary divided it, one piece for each hand. Now she had two fists full of bread with innards dropping out and she continued to bump into my elbow. Four times I helped to situate her in the chair. I finally said, "Mary! Sit squarely on your bottom and don't move. EAT your sandwich, and please stop bumping Mommy's arm!" Mary wanted to maintain her dignity and take the attention off her. She turned to Micah who was innocently sitting across from her and was oblivious to her situation. "Micah," she pronounced as if an intellectual psychologist wearing thick, wire-rimmed glasses, "I see YOU have a problem."

Mary and Becca's naïve ways were authentic not clownish. That is what made living with them so funny. One day when Trish the college intern was living with us, I overheard Mary ask, "Do you have hair in your pits?" She'd seen Jim and Nathan with their shirts off. My eyes shot open in horror. "Mary, come to Mommy right now," I said as steadily as possible. Mary crawled off the bed where Trish was reading and looked wide-eyed at me in the passageway. I put down the laundry basket and stooped to Mary's eye level.

"Mary, we don't ask people about things like that! It's not good manners. It might embarrass them."

Mary's eyes were filled with wonder. "Why?"

"Because…(I fished for words)…we just don't do that. It's not nice! Do you understand? I do not want you to ask anybody that question again." I had to stop lecturing because I could feel a bubble of laughter surfacing. I did not want to distract from the importance of the moment.

"OK!" The case was recorded in Mary's cerebral files. At dinner that night, it was Mary's turn to pray. She folded her two, chubby hands together and took a deep breath. "Thank you, God, for dis day, and dis food, and PLEASE help us not to talk about our pits! Amen!" I hope God was laughing during prayer, because we all were.

The importance of laughter in the house cannot be underestimated. Our family had to take a lot of hits in the solar plexus of life. Children, with all of their innocence and idiosyncrasies, balanced all these hurts with healthy therapies of laughter. They were the medicine that kept the family merry rather than morbid. That was why it was so critical that we have family time. We ministered to each other by simply enjoying one another, being a balm and cordial at the end of each day.

How delighted I was that we had six of these remedial bottles. Each one cured family ailments with his or her unique chemistry or soothed each other after the bumps and abrasions of hard knocks. Nathan was particularly cheerful about most everything. He saw the humor and constructive uses in our bumps and bruises. He laughed contagiously. Anne and Micah were straightforward about life. Good, bad, or ugly they told it like it was, garnished with dry wit and the bottom line approach. This was in itself funny. Meg simply enjoyed life and people and had a zest for fun. She helped us all participate rather than watch. Mary and Becca were two little pills on which we wanted an overdose.

Having fun was a priority with the kids. The biggest challenge was how to go about it. Because there was very little store-bought amusement available, they simply concocted their own fun whenever friends or circumstances opened wide the opportunity. Nathan and Harrison, with their homemade slingshots, pelted the poisonous blue head lizards that ran upon the wall fence. Micah and Ryan were often in the trees, staining their faces and hands and clothes with mulberries or eating guavas until their bellies puffed out. They also spent hours and days constructing Lego creatures and buildings. Fortunately, kids have fun with anything as simple as dirt and water. The little ones made mud pies and played market by selling grass, leaves, and stones to imaginary customers. Tag, capture the flag, hide-n-seek, water fights,

Micah providing comic relief

and wheelbarrow rides were new sports when the Fogles or the Bandas came over. The MK group we'd started was once-a-week fun and social connections with other MKs outside our mission group.

The absence of television or videos the first term did more for developing the kids' imagination and love for fun than any other single element. What appeared to be a handicap was actually a catapult to ingenuity. Without amusement crutches the children learned to walk on their own funny bones. They created games and even invented a new sport: roach killing. The Zambians called the two varieties of roaches Germans or Americans. The big fat ones they labeled the Americans; and the small fast ones were the Germans. Mary's first exposure to an American roach brought a bloodcurdling scream, terrorizing the antennae-waving American who was emerging from under the cupboard. She stood stiff in her tracks until her little arms trembled from tension, and Supermom had to fly in for the rescue. Becca exhaled her feelings in one long blast of crying and promptly passing out. At every sighting, there were gasps, stomps and shrieks, clearly indicating our level of affection for these invaders.

The roaches were bad everywhere, but the big house on Buluwe Road was like a leftover of the eleventh Egyptian plague. The nine septic pits, if not regularly treated, were black with the moving insects. We exterminated, scalded, and smashed roaches by the hundreds, but the invaders penetrated our defense lines. The children retaliated. This was the new sport. Some nights after supper, the children would gather in the center of the dark kitchen, shoes, swatters, and brooms in hand. At the signal, the light was switched on, and it was a race to see who could make it back to the cupboards alive, the kids or the roaches. Mary was right in the middle of the stampede, her Velcro sandal thumping and swatting with a vengeance. The squeals and screams mingled with glee and "git'im!" through the duration of the raid. At the end of the slaughter, the losers were swept into piles for deposit into the dust bins.

The enjoyment of life seemed to be activated by challenges and hardships. We had seen the children suffer some and at the time it hurt and concerned us. But for the most part, we found it made the children hardier and more flexible afterwards. It took sickness to help them appreciate health; loneliness to help them appreciate friends; separations to make them cling to family; and pressures to make them turn to God. As the children saw great poverty, they learned the value of their possessions. As we faced big problems, they witnessed the presence and capabilities of God to address those problems. We rounded the corner and headed for home realizing that we had been on a venture that had prospered the children. It had given them an advanced education, lessons beyond the textbooks and the rote answers to life. I was not sure all the children passed every class or assignment from God. I surely had not. But as parents we were awed by the resilience and endurance which they demonstrated.

If we were to return to Africa for another term we would never be able to duplicate the joys or trials or service that our entire family had lived out together. Nathan would be remaining for college, and maybe Anne would too. I also wanted time to stand still, if only for savoring a while longer, the joy I felt when I saw the children participating in Christianity rather than just observing it. Nathan and Megan were reaching friends with life-to-life impact, people like Sam and Harrison. The children were all responding to the needs around them with compassion and service. Anne loved teaching children; she was, in fact, teaching her siblings. One week she came home with this humorous incident: "I was reviewing the Bible story with the kids and said, 'So when Jesus was in the desert, who tempted Him? Does anyone know? Who tempted Jesus?' Rebecca, with front row enthusiasm, shot up her hand, 'I did it!'" That was just one of the joys of serving Jesus together!

I wanted to preserve these happy, hard experiences for us all. That was part of the reason for this book of remembrances. A few letters from the children, a poem from Micah, and Nathan's journal, *Chips (Chips of My Life)* helped put together pieces of their daily lives as the term was drawing to a close. Some are more than a hint at their anticipations of the homecoming in June.

Micah, fascinated by cars from the time he had his first matchbox model, had a whole different perspective of vehicles after being in Lusaka. His first-grade poem suggests some of his Zambian observations:

CARS

By Micah Chambers

Cars are fast and
Cars are slow.
I know how to
Make a car go.

Cars are green and
Cars are blue.
I'd like to drive
My dad's car too.

Some are strong,
And some are smashed.
Some you drive.
Others are trashed.

Excerpts from Anne's letters–age 15:

It seems as though we've only been here a couple of weeks on some days, and then on other days (like today), it seems as though we should be packing to leave in a few days. I'm so thankful that God doesn't change with all of our tossing emotions. Africa has been very good for me. I don't in the slightest bit miss the junky music, the television shows or commercials, or the peer pressure in clothing fads or general living. I haven't been hit with the homesickness I'd expected. God is faithful to provide for all of my needs.

Nathan and Sam

The Lord led about fifty kids to Himself from Chawama Bible Club. Aunt Sallie leads it, and we kids help. The enthusiasm is refreshing and amazing! There are still several new kids coming each Friday afternoon. It's just incredible!

Well, I have turned a year older and grown a few inches taller. My birthday was a happy day that seemed so unreal! We all went out to a nice restaurant as a family. The meal had its own comedian for us. Mary attempted in earnest to follow Mom's example and use her "good" table manners. You should have seen her chewing with her mouth closed!

PARENTHETICAL NOTE FROM MOM'S RECORDS: *Mary was our little 'Anne of Green Gables,' trying so hard to be a grown-up three-year-old. She sat on her knees in the chair, watching the family. She picked up her spoon and balanced her food all the way to her mouth. Then she closed her lips and imitated the jaw and lip action of a young camel chewing cud: her teeth never contacted each other. After a lumpy swallow and a wince, she asked for her approval rating, "Did I do it right, Mommy?" I choked out a, "Yes, dear," while the children silently laughed themselves to tears.*

A composite of two of Megan's letters—age 11:

Mr. Banda is a grandpa and he is only 37! I play with Mr. Banda's kids a lot. His oldest daughter had a baby about three months ago and she is the cutest little baby on earth. All the babies out here are adorable! Mr. Banda and Harrison are my best Zambian friends out here.

February 17, 1994

I have twenty days of school left. I should be done March 18ᵗʰ! [Meg was our over achiever.] *Can you believe it?!! Anne and Nathan hate me for it, not to mention that we are going to Harare in two weeks. So, we have to get ahead in school!*

I made Mary a dress! Can you believe it?!! I, me, myself made a dress! It actually even looks like a dress! It only took three days. I also

191

finished two cross stitches and just started a new one that is quite big. I have finished a lot of cross stitches since we came to Zambia.

Well, I have been filling space, and now my letter is getting very boring so I will leave you to RIP (rest in peace). How do you like the new saying? RIP. It sounds weird! Well, I am just being boring again so again I will leave you to RIP! Love, Megan

From *Chips (Chips of My Life)*
Nathan' Journal Entries:

March 20, 1994

I went running after a walk with the girls. As I was running through the fields at Ibex Hill, I was startled by a three-foot black snake lying across the path. Having just been at the snake farm in Zimbabwe, I was not going to check it out to see if it was a black mumba. I just hurdled it, adrenaline pumping, and booked it back to the house. I improved my time by nearly fifty seconds!

March 22, 23

Fogles dropped by this afternoon... I got to meet Ben today [college intern]. My first impression? Wow, he's shorter than me! And he looks young, too! He's not very talkative yet, still warming up, I suppose, but he seems like a real, nice guy! This afternoon was a blast.

Before dinner, Megan and I threw the baseball. I wasn't paying much attention to where I was walking and stepped right in a pile of dog poop. All over my heel! On top of that, Megan had trouble catching the ball, no matter what glove she used. Dinner tonight was pizza. I had six pieces.

April 12, 1994

Today was boring! I didn't do nothin! Blast! Now what am I supposed to write about?

Um... I went to school today. Nothing unusual. I had a really tough time getting' stuff done. Algebra was tough and L-O-N-G! I also had to write a history essay about the cold war that we had zilch resources to draw from. The dumb thing took me an hour and a half.

April 20, 1992

It's our last real, home school day. I'll miss wearing shorts and no shoes, but I really need a desk [already packed]. This afternoon after lunch, we all sat down and discussed how we'd handle certain aspects of life (T.V., visiting friends, dress) when we go back to the States so that they don't handle us. It was helpful, enjoyable, and needful. I even learned a few things! Life's great!

Tonight we had special McDonald's night, compliments of Mom. Man, were they good! Fantabulous! Then, after we all cleaned off the table, we played BOGGLE. I did terrible, but really didn't matter. I'd like to get some rest. Last night, I accidentally left a window open and so I had to go to mosquito smashing from 2:00–3:00 in the morning. Now I'm all drained out.

We got mail today. I got two things: a letter from Mr. Harkleroad [family friend/deacon from home church] and note from Rachel [cousin]. There was also a tape from Mohlers. It was, to say the least, refreshing to hear from them. Only forty-two days till we leave now.

Back to Anne, a letter from May 5, 1994:

Life is really great! I'm celebrating the fact that I'm nearly done with all my schoolwork. Yeah!

We were busy packing barrels yesterday... Everything has to be wrapped and rewrapped in order to avoid termite problems. Termites got into our container and ate up some Bibles and Sunday school materials. We're being extra careful now.

We're going to Lumbembe on Sunday. It's like our church's missionary work. We pay to send Bible school students down to preach. The people sit on logs, live in mud/straw houses, cook over open fires, etc. It will be a nice experience, and I look forward to the opportunity. [The morning we were to leave, Rebecca came down with a high fever, so Anne covered impromptu as children's teacher.]

193

Anne teaching in Village of Lumbembe

I think that I'm done teaching Sunday school. Mrs. Byrne [newest missionary, working with the Bells] is taking over my class. I can't get used to having a Saturday without Bible club and Sunday school to prepare for. Oh! Bible club is over for the school year. We had a great closing week, with five children saved. The kids had been coming all year, so they really understood and were ready. Seeing their belief is so encouraging and renewing!

*I've been doing a countdown of days since 63; we're currently at 28 . . . and counting. I'm ready to see my friends and family; to walk into a real store; to **sit in** a church service as a listener instead of a leader; to go for a walk without an escort/bodyguard; to attend a school with more than six students (and YES! I do look forward to the guys!!); to stand in a crowd without feeling one hundred pairs of eyes glued to my body . . . I'm ready to see London and head for home!*

We'll see you soon! Coming home this year seems to be on all of our minds, and we can't wait to be in your arms as we step off of the plane. We miss you! ONLY 23 DAYS FROM TODAY! It'll be great, and we'll have so much to talk about.

WE ARE COMING HOME!

Love, Anne

Chapter 26

Last Two Letters Home

Prayer Letter, May 1994, to churches and supporters:

Hey everybody! Ready or not, here we come!

We're counting down the last month! What's it like? Well, the excitement is about driving us crazy, not to mention mixed emotions. The ecstatic feelings of going home, combined with the sadness of leaving these people, are a tough combination to swallow. It's a little like trying to enjoy a grapefruit after brushing with Crest: the flavors are better enjoyed separately. Add to those feelings Africans dropping in for last visits; boxes, trunks, barrels, and "for sale" signs next to piles of keepers, ditch-its, and sellers; the weariness of decision making, the pressure of responsibilities, and our enthusiasm over new church growth. It's about as weird a combination as the food we're eating so that we can polish off last pantry supplies. It is this context that prompted my 5 a.m. comment: "Jim, let's just skip this month."

Yet it is this context that draws us back to basics, to more frequent periods of prayer and necessary renewal. The greater the threat of frenzy, the more urgent our desire to walk in the Spirit, not dash around in the flesh. This seems to be our present challenge. John Wesley said, "Though I am always in haste, I am never in a hurry because I never undertake more work than I can go through with calmness of spirit." Pray that we may live such well-ordered lives!

One thing that calms our minds as we leave is the steady progress within the church and its outreach. It is reassuring evidence that God has begun a good work and will continue it even in our absence. In April, thirteen new believers were baptized, and we enjoyed our first communion service as a church. Outreaches through soccer, ladies' Bible study, children's Bible club, and Zambians invitations are increasing our influence and attendance with over 100 last week. Incidentally, the request for Bible studies has been greater than our supplies. The Byrnes, who will replace us, have exciting potential but hard work before them. We're praying for them.

Once we are gone from Zambia, what are we looking forward to? We've been talking about that one. Top priority: seeing family and friends. After that?

Micah: smooth roads! Ice cream, a bicycle ride, churches with pews

Rachel: garage sales! Garbage pick up, bug-free staples, consistent electricity and water, libraries

Megan: shopping in real stores, horseback riding, youth group

Anne: variety! Different clothes, fried fish, snow

Jim: sports, no cement block walls, our own house, hard-shell tacos

Nathan: driving, sports, lawn mowers, my own room

Mary: Sunday School, new books, new friends

Until then, we continue to stock up on experiences: we camped out in the game reserve one night. On May 15th, we will be hosted by villagers in Lumbembe, our outreach ministry 2.5 hours south of Lusaka. Lumbembe is a small traditional village where the Bible school students and missionaries have a church start of about 30 believers. We're hoping the spiritual food we offer will be received and that the village menu will be digestible. (Gulp! Jim, where did you put those Tums?) We are happily adding to our ministry experience and memories, even as we close out our time here. Your prayers and notes encourage us to finish out strong.

As we reflect on the time here, we remember many of you and the significant influence you've had on us and this ministry. You are as much a part of our experience as the Zambians, the culture, and the varied circumstances. Thank you for teaming up with us. Our plans for further ministry are candidate school in July and full-time status; then, deputation for remaining support. We hope many of you will be able to continue our team effort. We are open for meetings, conferences, and invitations for American food! Let's get together!

We love you!
Jim and Rachel
Nathan, Anne, Megan, Micah, Mary, and Rebecca

Excerpts from a letter to my sisters, May 15, 1994:

This is Sunday. I'm supposed to be teaching the children at the village today while Jim is preaching to the adults, but last night Rebecca began vomiting, with fever, and diarrhea. I feel badly to have missed. It kind of fulfills my childhood image of me as Mary Slessor. Well, we should get a lot more of that next term.

I have had in my heart the desire to spend personal time with both of you for months. I asked myself an honest question: why do I seem to neglect writing the people I love the most?! After a lot of soul searching, I think I have an honest answer: I don't have much personal time. The little scraps of time are remnants that I piece together to have devotions or intimate time with Jim. I was complaining to the Lord about it last month, and I have now had several unusual times caring for sick kids or unexpected schedule changes that have given me minimal regrouping time... Ministry is like an ever-present, slow leak. Before long, I'm flat without realizing my own needs were unattended (pumping up time).

One thing that I wanted to share with you was my scrape with death last week. I wrote about it to myself, and decided to enclose a copy.

I have hesitancy about sharing it, as some criticize me for walking in the mornings alone. I crave the quiet, regrouping time. The house is so small that there are no quiet corners. I think I ought to let the Lord's mercies be known, so that you may give Him adequate thanks on our behalf… so I share from my journal.*

I feel the results of prayer for me. I can sense a unique closeness as the Lord draws near me. I need it in times like these: I have to AGAIN leave people I love and a work that God Himself has developed. Being separated tears me up.

We requested a special meeting of the missionaries to discuss possibilities for the future of the field and ministry. We met over parts of two days to brainstorm and to unveil our personal interests for the future. It was helpful in seeing whether we can fit in and be a contribution to this field. Before the meeting, we were trying to reason on a lot of ambiguity. I'm so glad Jim was firm about remaining home on furlough for two years. That will give time to confirm the decision to return, plus give the kids some American social growth, time with family, and time to get Nathan and Anne in college. Meanwhile, I wonder how the grace of God will provide "homes" for them while we are in Zambia, or how I will live without them "available." Being out here together has drawn us closer than if we'd lived stateside.

Rebecca has fallen back to sleep, and since I slept very little last night, I want to rest some. I just fight it because sleep seems like such a waste of this good time.

I long to see you. I think of you every day.
Rach

* * *

*Account retold from my journal entry, May 6, 1994:

I woke up this morning at about five and went for a walk at about 6:15. (I was very downcast about facing all the goodbyes, separations, and an uprooted life again.) I jogged onto Twin Palm Road, past the Baptist Seminary, to the first house and then turned around. Upon coming back, I decided to pick a bouquet of black-eyed Susans for the breakfast table. They were at the edge of the old cemetery road. I have always had an intrigue with reading epitaphs, so I decided to go a short ways down the dirt road under the beautiful trees, eyeing a few of the grave markers as I walked. A man was far ahead of me. I was alone otherwise, but in "safe" and clear view of Twin Palm Road. As I looked at the tombstones, I heard footsteps on the road behind me. A tall, young man, poorly dressed, seemed to be following me. He caught up with me. I greeted him and let him pass. He asked me where I was going. I (naively) answered, "I'm just going for a walk." Then, so as not to be on the road with him, I pretended to show interest in a grave about twenty feet off of the dirt path. It was enough to keep a healthy distance between us and to allow me to get out of his view so that I could now turn around and slip back toward the main road.

When he was maybe fifty yards ahead of me, I began walking back toward Twin Palm Road. Again I heard footsteps coming up quickly behind me. I knew it was the man, and I was beginning to flood with adrenaline. I felt my personal space being violated. Somewhere in my past, I had always determined that if ever I was mugged from behind, I would turn and face my attacker, eyeball to eyeball. I wanted him to remember that I had a face and that I had seen him before he killed me. At this point, all that I had "pre-lived" in my imagination clicked in, as if on auto-pilot.

I whirled around suddenly and faced the man. Both hands held a sharp, curved grass sickle at about eye level. It was raised to strike me. My sudden movement startled us both. I had not seen the grass sickle as a weapon before, and he had only seen a victim's back. I felt deep, penetrating FEAR as we stared at each other. He looked like a man in a trance, like he was driven without thought or conscience.

"What are you DOING?!" I shot out an intense, adrenaline filled question. (As if I didn't know!)

He stopped moving. Looking at the cutter in his hands, and back at my face, the "trance look" broke. He looked like he'd snapped out of it and had come to the realization of his crime. The sickle lowered as he said, "Sorry, Madam! Sorry! I was just going this way!" He pointed to a tiny footpath between the graves on the other side of the road, down from where we were standing. Then he took off running, as if frightened by his own insanity.

As he did, my adrenaline raised my decibels a few more notches, "Well, you'd BETTER BE GOING!"

I now had to walk back down the cemetery road and return home without appearing to be shaken. If the man was watching from behind the trees or tombstones, I felt I needed to look "together." This was not so easy. My bones turned to jello, and tears began to leak out as I realized the life-threatening circumstances from which I had been delivered. I wiped my eyes with the back of my hand, in a pretense that I had dirt in them.

I had an argument with myself all the way home. Should I tell anyone about this? If I did, Jim might never let me out of his sight again! He was so protective, and I so craved private time.

However, it didn't seem right to hide anything from him. I'd never done that before. The debate between my perspectives was strong, as the poor posies in my grasp would testify.

I stepped inside the gate, clutching my flowers. By this time, I had talked myself out of telling anyone. Banda had just arrived for work. He greeted me, "Muli Bwanji!"

I was supposed to say, "Ndili bwino," but I could not, so I responded, "Bwino, but I…" At that point, I began to break down. All the adrenaline from fear had to have an outlet. I briefly explained while crying that I was all right, only badly frightened. This statement was not convincing. I dashed for the laundry house at the back of the property to get control of myself. Mr. Banda followed me. Kind Mr. Banda!

He peppered me with questions. Avoiding these was not successful. He insisted that I get the keys to Tin Lizzy and Pastor Chambers, and we track this guy down. I was thinking like an American. What good would that do? I didn't have a scratch on me. It was over twenty minutes ago. We'd never find him. I was not harmed physically, and I had nothing but my word against his—if we were to take the case to the police. Banda did not give up easily. He was thinking like an African: we needed to teach this guy a lesson!

"How are we going to do that? He's long gone by now! I told you he took off down the path between the graves!" I argued.

Without batting an eye he said, "I will catch him myself. We will tie him up and drag him behind the car down the road." My eyeballs stood on their stems.

"We will not! That is TERRIBLE! It would take his skin off! It could kill him!"

"Yes!" Banda was firm. "We have to teach these guys a lesson! They can't just go killing people for their tennis shoes." That was the only valuable I had on me, other than an old dime in my pocket.

My horror at this sense of justice was helping me gain composure. I closed the discussion and begged him not to tell Jim. Banda was ticked at me. He helped me hang out the jeans on the line, and then stayed in the wash room to cool off. I washed my puffy eyes and red nose. When I returned to the house, I put the flowers in water, walked upstairs, and reported the whole thing to Jim. I never could, nor would, keep a secret from him. I closed my journal entry, "I give thanks to the Lord that I am ALIVE, and that someone prayed for my safety today. 'He shall give His angels charge over thee, to keep thee.'"[1]

The next day was Mother's day. I did not tell the children until later why that day was extra special, why all their cards and love brought tears to my eyes, and why they meant more than usual to me.

Chapter 27

Long Goodbyes and Sweet Gifts

Much of the last two weeks of May were marked by sad goodbyes. A stream of Zambian friends stopped by the house while we packed and sorted, either bringing gifts of remembrance or asking for them. Some brought sweet cards with messages of appreciation, and some sacrificed above their means to send us off with special gifts. I had not realized the significance of these gifts until it became obvious that everyone expected more than a hug or handshake at our parting. They expected us to stop, visit, and reminisce over our relationship and the separation to come. It took a great deal of time and concentration, especially in the midst of the clamor of our family packing and the disarray of the house. In the United States, departures meant people offered to *help*; out of respect for the deadline of departure, they made *brief* farewells. Here, it was long goodbyes that helped communicate the affection and value of the relationship. This new discovery certainly added stress to our still-American way of viewing a tight schedule. Why did it feel like we were sliding down the learning curve again?

Sallie and Larry understood our time constraints and helped, and then they helped some more. We stayed in their home the last week of transition. "Aunt Sallie" cared for the little ones, cooked, and pulled me back together every night when we arrived for supper. Their enablement was consistent with the friendship they had exemplified all term. As teammates, we were first and foremost friends. Others on the team had chosen us as friends as well, and they helped with food or whatever we needed. Enough cannot be said about their value and ministry of encouragement.

One notable but unexpected visitor pulled into the yard to give us quite a significant gift "in appreciation for our help." It was not a Zambian; it was our British conductor for the Lusaka Music Society. He and his wife—Megan's piano teacher—had determined to help us enjoy England by arranging an all-paid, half-day tour of London. I was stunned at this man's generosity. My contributions to the Society had been so small compared to his, that I knew this was more than appreciation for Anne's, Megan's, and my participation in the music community. I would like to believe that it was an unspoken respect that he had for our faith. He himself had become a spiritual skeptic, so when our chamber orchestra performed holy works, such as *Messiah*, he looked to me for some measure of credibility. In the spring performance, I auditioned for a solo which I wanted to sing as my farewell testimony to the orchestra and audience: "I Know That My Redeemer Liveth." The conductor had already determined that the regular soprano soloist would be performing this, as she was quite capable. She was a voice coach from the London School of Music. When I auditioned for the piece, he gave it to me, saying, "I have changed my mind about letting N. sing this. I know she can do it well. She's done it several times. However, I think…I think…you will make it *believable*." I think this man's gift was a token of the respect he had for our entire family's faith. It has been a memory to which I return with awe and gratitude.

The last Sunday with our church was most difficult for me to hold together emotionally. Each of the church members represented a relationship, a memory, a gift of grace. After Jim preached his farewell message, the people began to come forward and share testimonies of what we meant to them and how we would be missed. The Viyolas were last, presenting two very special gifts from the whole church, a copper clock for Jim and an embroidered suit for me. Both gifts were a sacrifice of others so that we could have their best. We were blessed by such kindness, but they were more blessed because they gave so selflessly. We received these gifts with two hands, even as they were offered—a sign of mutual honor and gratitude one for the other.

The eldest children had formed stronger bonds with their friends over the past year. Megan and Harrison had many connections with others, but their own relationship trumped them all. Their companionship had been like brother and sister, almost inseparable. Special gifts were exchanged to remember their friendship. Anne had at last linked with a girl about her age: Angela. Angela was bright, with a smile that lit up her face. She lived with her aunt so that she could attend the city schools. She attended my girls' class on Saturdays, as well as Bible club, teen class, and church. That spring, she began to gravitate towards Anne's friendship. One day they were walking along the road talking, and Angela slipped her hand into Anne's, a gesture that thrilled Anne's heart even if it was awkward to our way of expressing friendship. She'd wanted a Zambian friend this whole term. Angela's remembrance gift, a pair of earrings, and her farewell notes gave Anne hope for future growth in their relationship.

Nathan's relationship with Sam stood heads over the others. As we prepared for our departure, he learned that Sam had wanted to try out for the Under 20's soccer team, but one requirement was shoes, and Sam was a barefoot footballer. He did not have the resources to produce these, either. Nathan had two pairs of soccer cleats: his old, getting-tight pair, and a pair that Jim had purchased for him to grow into. The second was nice leather, and barely worn, as Nathan had to stuff toilet paper into the toes to keep his foot from sliding forward. Nathan asked our permission to give these to Sam. He cleaned them up, tied them together with the laces, and handed them to Sam one Saturday.

"I don't know if these will fit you, but *if* they fit, you are more than welcome to them."

Sam was not a demonstrative person, but he was genuine. He received them with both hands, holding them on the palms of his hands as if they were breakable. Still holding them with both hands, he looked in awe at Nathan. "Oh! Thank you!"

"You're welcome!" Nathan responded enthusiastically.

When Sam turned to take his treasure home, he never held them by the laces. He kept them in both hands, the way the Christmas cards depict the wise men carrying gold, frankincense, and myrrh. Sam made the team before we left for the United States. Going to practice in his new shoes was a dream come true. However, one of his first games was on Sunday morning. Sam told the coach, "I will not be there. I go to church on Sundays." And he did. As much as Sam loved football, his first love for God was the sweetest farewell gift received.

June 2nd was the day of departure. The airport scene was far more difficult than we had anticipated. Separation was emotionally tearing for all of us—them and us. I cried with Larry; I cried with Sallie; Sallie was having the same struggles with words that I had. It seemed that neither one of us felt compelled to talk. We understood each other without verbiage. A simple note expressed her heart. Then I took turns with the family crying with Sherry. She had baked us her famous zucchini bread, and thrust this into my already full arms. Even Mr. Banda had come to the airport. He was all dressed in his Sunday best, a grey suit from Jim with a bright red shirt and Jim's hand-me-down tie. Poor Mr. Banda! He looked so lost there, and he couldn't seem to think of something beyond rote to say, "Have a safe journey, Madam." He wasn't really speaking when he talked; he was speaking more with his soft, sad eyes and warm handshake. We had entrusted so much of our family to his care, and he had rarely let us down. He was almost a daily part of our family life.

Once we passed through the check-in section, we could only wave to everyone through the glass. They were all waiting on the stairway until our plane took off. Our family of eight caught attention: eight members, twenty three pieces of luggage. The two little girls sat on the luggage trolley, perched on Nathan's suitcases. Becca held Ellie, the pink pachyderm, by the neck.

The protocol for leaving the country was long enough to bore the little ones: crankiness and hunger set in. As we climbed the broken escalator for the departure lounge, everyone was losing something. Two stairs from the top, Mary lost her shoe to the bottom of the escalator; Bec lost her patience to an empty stomach, and some were still losing composure because this field trip was coming to an end. It was terrible and wonderful all mixed up.

In the departure lounge, we broke into the zucchini loaf until the boarding call. The parade of eight marched all over again, down the stairs and out to the bus that would take us to the plane. In the brief moment from the terminal to the bus, we heard Fogles, Sherry, Harrison and Mr. Banda yelling in unison, "Goodbye, Chambers!" We threw a windmill wave to the observation deck before entering the bus, and kept waving from the top of the plane steps, though we could only see their silhouettes.

Chapter 28

Reentry

The window seat was mine on the flight to London. I looked down thousands of feet below to the clouds thinking, "I miss Africa!" I could hardly believe how attached I had become in this short span of time. The kind words and many farewell scenes replayed pleasantly on my mental video. The children slept well, but certainly not for the duration of the thirteen-hour flight. We had "plane breakfast" before landing in London.

Reentry into the London airport was shocking. The pace of life instantly quickened; as did the reality check that we were no longer in third-world conditions. I wasn't sure I liked it at first, now that I had adjusted to the other world. I sensed the value changes of the culture immediately: progress and punctuality were rigid priorities; flexibility to people, not so much.

We were to spend our overnight layover at a bed and breakfast guesthouse, the Foreign Mission Society. Getting eight of us there in London taxis, hand luggage and all would have cost as much as the overnight accommodations, But our Father, Who always travels with us, had prepared everything in advance. The Lusaka Music Society conductor had arranged a private tour bus to meet us at the airport. We spotted the guide's placard "WELCOME CHAMBERS" as we entered the reception area. I had no idea that God had arranged such a smooth and accommodating reception before we could even think of it. The guide was a warm-hearted Irishman, who knew the airport and London "like the back of his hand," as he described it.

That morning, we visited every and any site, most of which we never even knew about. This man had a fascination with history, and told each site's story as if he'd lived during that era personally. We saw everything from regal and royal to Westminster Abbey and Scotland Yard. It was intriguing enough to stave off sleep for the first two hours, but my personal exhaustion threatened to take over. Seeing my drowsiness in his overhead mirror, he asked if there were any sites we wanted more than others. I said, "I've always wanted to see Spurgeon's chapel and the cemetery where Susanna Wesley and John Bunyan are buried." The guide's eyes confirmed his private shock at my unusual requests, but he knew exactly where they were and how to get us there. As we drove, he confessed he knew very little about the history of these places, though he did know about the dissenter's cemetery. We had opportunity to share a small bit of our faith and spiritual heritage with him as we drove across the city.

Arriving at Wesley's chapel, he parked the bus and told us to take as much time as we wanted. He wanted a smoking break. The chapel and Susanna Wesley's monument intrigued me as a mother. This woman was "just a mother" (did I mention of nineteen children?), a "mere housewife" who laid down her life and ambitions for husband and children, and I was here with my own family paying tribute to that example. She probably died without ever knowing she would be renowned for her simple, focused life to God and home, that someone would erect a monument in her honor long after hardships and fatigue were finished. This made a deep impression on me. "Those who honor Me I will honor."[1]

Across the street from the chapel was the dissenter's graveyard. In all of London, this was my favorite place. In this ancient plot were buried the heroes from my personal hall of fame. "How I would love to watch this place on resurrection day! These are the 'ones of whom the world was not worthy.'"[2]

I drank in the names and epitaphs of men and women with living faiths, men whom the world's "church" rejected, but who were accepted in the Beloved. Many of their epitaphs were weathered beyond legibility, but their names still identified their selflessness, martyrdom and faithful, fervent love for God. I had my picture taken next to John Bunyan's grave, my hero since my tenth birthday. This was when my parents gave me the children's version of *Pilgrim's Progress*. It did not occur to me until later that Bunyan—like my Jim—was a tinker, a simple jack-of-all-trades. God had used him mightily, once he was a broken vessel.

The guide was getting anxious to move on. We still had to visit Spurgeon's chapel, and it was almost thirty minutes further, so we left the cemetery to board our bus. I was refreshed spiritually and energized physically by my time in the cemetery. Those being dead yet spoke to me; they were a great cloud of witnesses urging a tired me to get up and press on. By the time we reached Spurgeon's chapel, I had received my second wind, so to speak. Again, I was encouraged to consider what great things God could do with little people.

That afternoon we rested at the grand, old house of the Foreign Mission Club. Just before supper, we decided to take a quiet, family stroll. There was a lovely park, we were told, just down the street. Standing at the end of the street, we waited for traffic so we could cross into the park. A young woman stepped from behind us into the street, her head down, totally lost in thought and oblivious to a public transport bus which was mere meters from us. The driver was alert, and tried to swerve to avoid hitting her, but it was impossible. The woman was thrown into an airborne spiral and struck her head on the pavement just meters from where we stood. Instinctively I rushed to her side, hearing Jim caution from behind, "Rach! Don't get involved!" He knew my compassion took over, and there were others in this place that could tend to her. I was not as "needed" here as in Africa. This was another reentry awakening.

The woman was still conscious, though showing signs of the head injury and shock that was setting in. I reassured her that help would be coming, to lie still, and other encouragements to keep her with us. A nurse, on her way home from work, was on the bus and able to take over until an ambulance and the police arrived. We sent the children ahead to the park with Nathan while we waited to give an eye-witness report to the authorities. By the time they had taken the information, our children had returned to the mission club housing, and we were freezing in the cool, evening air. So much for the quiet, family walk!

The next day, our London tour guide returned with our private bus to take us to the airport. I do not know if this was something he volunteered to do, or if our Lusaka conductor had also paid for this. Either way, it was huge, and again showed that God provided *everything* we needed. The tour guide would not even accept a tip from us, but he did accept a tract!

The remaining eight-hour flight to O'Hare airport was too close to home for me to really sleep. The adrenaline was pumping, triggered by fresh thoughts of home and families we loved waiting there for us. I might have dozed some, but my mind was not restful. I was swinging like a pendulum between heaven and earth with prayers and wonderings about the people we'd left behind and the family we anticipated seeing again. The plan was for my family to meet us at the Chicago airport, and then for us to visit the Chambers' side in New York State the next week.

When the wheels of the plane touched down in America, the passengers broke into soft applause, perhaps grateful that the flight was at last over. Some made comments about how good it was to be home again. The thought puzzled me momentarily. Was this home for me, or wasn't it?

Getting through immigrations, customs, and baggage claims could not be hurried and was clearly not fast enough for any of us. When we were finally ready, Jim led the parade of trolleys. Rebecca sat solemnly in the luggage trolley wearing my African hat and clutching Ellie, her pink stuffed elephant, taking in this new world. Mary sat like queen of the trunks upon Anne's luggage as we came through the double doors into the reception lounge. Micah was about fifty-percent eyeballs,

My mom and dad

searching for his cousins. Before we could focus, we heard an outburst, a cheer and then applause. Our eyes followed the ruckus to balloons and a waving poster board that announced, "Welcome Home Chambers." I couldn't believe the fanfare was from my family! As soon as we cleared the restricted area, arms were all around us, and happy tears released.

I checked Rebecca to see how she was taking the change. She sat silently under my hat, just looking. Dad tried to make Becca smile. Mom said something grandmotherish, and Becca just looked poker faced, holding onto Ellie. "That's Gramma Mayo, Becca," I explained. "It's ok. This is MY mommy and daddy!" No one forced themselves upon Becca. She quickly connected the dots by observing our interactions with the new faces and soon defrosted her emotions for pictures.

The sights of the new world and the wealth of America began to draw my attention too. At the airport, I now took note of the flush toilets and running water, the perfect tiles, and the automated hand driers that worked. The van that pulled up to load our luggage seemed back-wards: the steering column was on the wrong side. Vehicles around us seemed too perfect. They were not even scratched, much less maimed, blowing smoke, or barely holding together. No one was piled into them or spilling out of them. As we drove to my sister's house, I marveled at simple things, like lawn mowers instead of grass slashers, driving on the right side of the road, professional-looking businesses, and fast food restaurants. It wasn't like I'd had amnesia; I'd simply disconnected from it. I'd learned a different set of expectations in Africa, and America did not fit these. I enjoyed turning on lights and finding electricity, or going into stores and finding variety and quality merchandise. Price tags actually meant what the item cost, and if I did not like it, I could not barter with the cashier. I was surprised at how much of Africa remained with me.

Within the first few days, Paul (our former pastor and now the president of Evangelical Baptist Mission) and Grace Jackson met us in Chicago. That reunion was sweet as well as stimulating. Paul used the time to share his counsel about indigenizing the work in Africa. It was excellent and proved to be time worthy. He never seemed to waste an opportunity to encourage us, and our respect for him made his seedling advice transplant into our church-planting philosophy.

The first week back, we made our way to New York, reconnecting with relatives and friends on the way. I felt a jolt every time I saw people who did not look the way I'd left them two years prior. There were plenty of people-shocks along our circuit ride. When we finally reached Mom and Dad Chambers, I felt like we were coming home. Mom and Dad didn't ever change much. Mom sang to herself in the kitchen, or rocked grandchildren, or found something to give away. Dad was always in work clothes, helping fix something or someone's problem. I had missed them so! Both had prayed and loved and thought about us so much. With them, we could pick up just where we had left off, and that was with strong hugs. Jim's emotions were most evident as he embraced his parents, long and hard. Dad and I hugged so intensely that tears leaked out both our eyes. One of the greatest blessings in missions was the support of our families. Jim's siblings and their families joined us at different times throughout the week, as their schedules would allow. They seemed so very protective and proud of Jim, happy and loyal in a way that could not be replaced by others who are not family.

Our last stop in New York was at Les' home, a rural village in the hills of the Southern Tier. Summer had not come to West Clarksville that year. I froze to the bone in the cold front that had settled in. What did warm me was the love there. Les was close in heart and prayers for Jim, and his small but loyal congregation reflected well his passion to be supportive. Their genuine interest for the ministry and their sacrificial giving was evidence of their faith and enthusiasm for in God to provide for us through them. They took missions seriously. They treated us like heroes, but when Jim got into the pulpit, he broke down emotionally. He knew how small and insufficient we were to think anything of ourselves. Our only greatness was being connected to God Himself through their prayers. Their responsiveness encouraged us, particularly when Jim was about to make a decision about whether to return to Zambia as career missionaries.

The final reentry was back to The Living Room in Cedarville. We pulled into the driveway, and eight pairs of eyes were on the house. *"We're home!"* I announced to myself and the family. It looked better than it ever had before. This was not only because it was home; it was because the church family had prepared the place inside and out for our occupancy. A welcome home sign hung on the door with a helium balloon tied to the porch light. There were freshly-planted flowers, stocked cupboards, and loaded refrigerator and freezer—more than their capacity could hold. Having just gone through a time of scarcity, having a fresh view of poverty, this abundance and generosity was overwhelming! The church people showed up soon after our arrival to move in furniture and bring greetings or meals or bags of clothes for the children. How the Lord knew our needs and met every one!

Anne had returned with one dress which was not wearing Africa on it. We had not realized how soiled and faded we had become until returning to a place of more pristine standards.

Our first Sunday in church, our new pastor, David Graham, recognized us before the congregation, welcoming us home with applause and words of appreciation. These kindnesses made us sense afresh our smallness and God's great mercies to us in this high calling. This church that sent us out was the church that *stayed with us* the entire term. I looked at this family of God around us: the women who had packed our bags for the field (I called them Mary Poppins, for their extraordinary ability to condense a roomful of supplies into one bag), the people who corresponded, the people who gave extra so that we could stay, the St. Clairs who visited us, the people who interceded in prayers, and the people who met needs and had passions for expanding the Church of Jesus Christ. This was our team, our family, our church. We really felt it would have been just as fitting for the eight of us to give them a standing ovation.

After the service, Pastor and Carol Graham took us to Cracker Barrel Restaurant so that we could get acquainted with one another. We were most grateful for the personal effort and interest they took to initiate the relationship. We certainly wanted that, but were ministry-tired and initially too overwhelmed to initiate much ourselves. Pastor Graham and Carol were warm-hearted southerners who specialized in making others feel important to them. They minimized the newness of our relationship by acceptance of us rather than analysis of us. This was from the Lord and opened us to their shepherding in our lives.

The next weeks we reconnected with everything from phone to neighbors to school enrollment. It took some time to settle back into our house and old routines and relationships. While others still loved us, we could not immediately find our place in their lives. They had gone on without us, even as we had to go on without them. So returning to the way things were did not actually fit as it used to. The children expressed some initial anxieties about feeling left out, but the Lord helped us keep perspective until the natural course of relationships had time to grow again.

Actually, the American friendships were so much more natural to us, now that we were in our own culture. At least we knew what to expect. Mary was only four, but she was already taking in the different social expectations and cultural etiquette. Children here were more closely supervised and did not play as roughly as the children in the poor neighborhoods where we ministered. She had more toys here and playgrounds and fascinating things to do. One day I took the younger children to a special kids' farm. There was a petting pen, a picking place, and a barn with a rope swing and slide from the haymow to hay pile. Since we were some of the first to arrive, we had the slide to ourselves. Mary no sooner reached the bottom but what her feet took off for the steps to go again. She was maximizing on fun, and I was tanking up on her laughter!

About ten o'clock, several school buses from an inner city school arrived. One whole classroom of children ran impulsively toward the barn. They had visited there before and clearly wanted the swing and slide and petting pen and EVERYTHING for themselves, just as Mary had. In their childlike abandon, they were oblivious to a little girl who was living with new-found freedom in a newly discovered world. They engulfed her and took over. Mary was pushed aside at the top of the slide, and she did not appreciate it. This was a little too much like that other world she'd just come from.

Without warning, she put her hands on her hips and looked at me indignantly. "WHO invited the Zambians here?" she erupted. My eyes ejected out of their sockets before I whisked her into my arms. It was so unexpected that I couldn't help laughing. I guess our four-year-old missionary had worn a bit thin on the edges. Fortunately, no one here was going to understand that statement, but a parent who knew its context. As we reconnected, we all recognized we needed some retreading. Our bald spots were still showing.

217

Chapter 29

Back On The Couch

Back in The Living Room, the couch did not feel the same. We did not fit quite as comfortably, though the cushions felt softer than before. We had experienced change. This Living Room was a cocoon into which we no longer fit. We were becoming different, something better suited for God's plan. This becoming process was not yet complete, but God had been giving us wings, and with our wings came an irreversible change. There was no turning back—no turning back into a caterpillar.

Jim and I had some decisions to make. Jim in particular turned to God about where our wings should take us. Zambia was certainly in our hearts, but again Jim questioned if his abilities should be placed into a hands-on ministry serving in construction, yet it seemed that God had presented him with a new kind of construction project, building up His Church. He liked it, but he felt so new and inexperienced in it; and he missed the everyday hammer-and-tool ministry. So he needed time with God to help him know what to do next. What was God making of us? During the time that he struggled with his own instincts and the reality of God's call into mission service, we applied for candidate school.

I had questions of my own. Having tasted the life of a Zambian, I knew I wanted more of it. The changes God was making in me were also irreversible. I loved these people, and that drew me back daily in thought and desire to be with them. My thoughts migrated in one direction, but Jim had to determine himself if this was to be our course. Becoming all things, I was beginning to see changes in myself. One thing I was becoming was sensitive to the struggles of the orphans and widows, the oppressed, and those afflicted with HIV. My eyes had been opened to pandemic death and its toll upon families, and—in particular—the greater Family of God. I was deeply concerned about the suffering in the church of Jesus Christ! But what was I supposed to DO about that? I wanted to make a difference, to be a help, to encourage and strengthen The Family, but how? The odds were so impossible to think about.

But God had just done something impossible. He was making us into something we could not design, imagine, or naturally accomplish on our own. He was changing us. The prophet Jeremiah mused over this kind of change when he said, "Can the leopard change his spots or the Ethiopian his skin?"[1] The question was redundant. The kind of change going on in us was a God thing. Our lives were personal witnesses that He was making a plumber and his family into missionaries. What had once seemed impossible was becoming reality.

That fact excited us. We could not sit back down on the couch complacently. All eight of us had been permanently affected by life in the ministry, yet each one had to respond to the work God called them to do. Nathan was talking about a mission's major in college, and Anne's heart and vision followed the same track. Megan bore clear evidence that cross-cultural change was in her spiritual DNA, though where God would use it was yet to be determined. The younger ones had accepted our summons as their own, and for this we were most grateful. They were all in-process, becoming what God had ordained them to be. Though none of us knew the outcome, we did know that He was not finished with us yet.

Charles Spurgeon summed up our thoughts in his little devotional, *Cheque Book of the Bank of Faith*, responding to the following verse: "The Lord will perfect that which concerns me; Your mercy, O Lord, endures forever; Do not forsake the works of Your hands."[2]

He who has begun will carry on the work which is being wrought within my soul. The Lord is concerned about everything that concerns me. All that is now good, but not perfect; the Lord will watch over, and preserve, and carry out to completion. This is a great comfort. I could not perfect the work of grace myself. Of that I am quite sure, for I fail every day, and have only held on as long as I have because the Lord has helped me. If the Lord were to leave me, all my past experience would go for nothing, and I should perish from the way. But the Lord will continue to bless me. He will perfect my faith, my love, my character, my life-work… He never leaves a work unfinished; this would not be for His glory, nor would it be like him. He knows how to accomplish his gracious design, and though my own evil nature, and the world, and the devil all conspire to hinder him, I do not doubt his promise. He will perfect that which concerneth me, and I will praise him forever.[3]

* * *

> *"No matter what accomplishments are made,*
> *somebody helped you."*
>
> —Placard at Disney World

My Somebodies

Writing a book for the first time can only happen once. I had no idea how much work was involved or the Somebodies who would be there to help me. I have now learned, and give grateful praise to God for those who were on my team.

My husband was my primary encourager. Jim sacrificed much for this project to become ours, not just mine. My love and appreciation for him go beyond words. Our children, their families, our siblings, and our parents have been my cheerleaders and my pray-ers so that our story could be shared. I am grateful that they are characters in the story just as they have been participators in its publication.

Eleanor Taylor is a friend who sticks close and loves well. She has done everything short of feeding me intravenously to get this book done: prayed, prepared meals, given me her apartment for writing, supplied chocolate, proofread and edited the manuscript unthinkable times. Without her practical friendship and encouragement, I would not have attempted such a project. I am thankful every time I think of her.

Pam (Dalby) Green is a long-time friend and Aunt Pam to my kids. She has been in our lives from college to wedding to children and then throughout our ministry. She has understood and participated in the vision for Zambia, visiting the field and using her professional skills to support us in our calling. She just happens to be a photographer and graphic artist. Her eye for who we are and making that image real is why I trusted her completely with the cover design, book layout, and overall presentation. I am most grateful for the investment she and her husband, John, have made in our family.

God sent Donna Messenger to our home just as this book was being completed. As a companion in the kingdom, missionary, and editor, she instinctively gave advice and editorial direction. In doing so, she became a newfound friend.

Sue Beikert was my inspiration to publish. As a long-time supporter and friend, she has encouraged me by believing that others would want to read our story. I am indebted to her for sharing her vision, enthusiasm, and hope for the book.

My highest praise is to the Lord Who enabled me to write down this story and surrounded me with help to have it published. May any appreciation for its content be directed to Him.

* * *

Notes

1. Malachi 3:16 (AMP).

Chapter 1: Our Open Door

1. Thomas, Major W. Ian, *The Indwelling Life of Christ* (Sisters, Oregon: Multnomah Publishers, 2006).

2. Psalm 48:14 (KJV).

3. Ephesians 2:10 (KJV).

Chapter 2: In the Living Room

1. I Corinthians 1:26–29 (NKJV).

2. I Corinthians 4:1–2 (KJV).

3. I Timothy 3:1 (KJV).

4. Exodus 4:10 (AMP).

5. Isaiah 52:10 (NKJV).

6. I Thessalonians 5:24 (KJV).

Chapter 3: Out of the Living Room

1. Matthew 4:19 (KJV).

Chapter 4: New Images

1. "Please Don't Send Me to Africa," words by Scott Wesley Brown & Phil McHugh, 1989 (BMG Songs, Inc./Pamela Kay Music/River Oaks Music).

2. Proverbs 16:9 (NKJV).

Chapter 5: Intentions and Plans

1. Isaiah 55:8, 9 (KJV).

2. Matthew 16:18 (KJV).

3. I Corinthians 3:9 (KJV).

4. I Corinthians 3:10, 11 (KJV).

5. John 10:27 (KJV).

6. Isaiah 41:13 (NKJV).

7. Bennett, Arthur G., *The Valley of Vision: A Collection of Puritan Prayers & Devotion* (East Peoria, Illinois: Versa Press, Inc., 2005).

8. "All the Way My Savior Leads Me" lyrics written in 1875 by Fanny J. Crosby (1820-1915) to a tune written by the Baptist minister Dr. Robert Lowry.

Chapter 6: Awe We Awmost Theya?

1. I Thessalonians 5:18 (KJV).

Chapter 7: Closing Doors Behind Us

1. Mark 10:29, 30 (KJV).

Chapter 8: No Turning Back

1. Luke 12:15b (NKJV).

Chapter 9: Launchings

1. Hebrews 13:5 (NKJV).

Chapter 11: And Just Who Is My Neighbor?

1. Matthew 5:43 (NKJV).

2. Matthew 5:46 (NKJV).

3. Matthew 25:35, 36, 40 (NKJV).

4. Matthew 25:40 (NKJV).

5. Matthew 5:42-47 (NKJV).

Chapter 12: Lessons

1. Psalm 103:2 (KJV).

Chapter 13: A Tea Party for Aliens

1. Mohler, Linda, "Out of Your World," music and lyrics used with permission).

Chapter 14: In My Dreams

1. John 1:14 (KJV).

Chapter 15: Coming Up for Air

1. Psalm 23:3 (NKJV).

Chapter 16: And Here Is Your Change

1. Isaiah 65:24 (KJV).

2. Bennett, Arthur G., *The Valley of Vision: A Collection of Puritan Prayers & Devotions* (East Peoria, Illinois: Versa Press, Inc., 2005).

3. "Be Still My Soul" (Finlandia), written by Katarina Von Schlegle b. 1697, translated by Jane L. Borthwick., scripture reference found in Psalm 46.

Chapter 17: When I Get Big

1. Psalm 16:8 (NKJV).

2. II Corinthians 3:18 (NKJV).

3. Hebrews 12:2 (KJV).

Chapter 18: Stung by Death

1. I Corinthians 15:55 (KJV).

2. Thomas, W. Ian, *The Indwelling Christ* (Sisters, Oregon: Multnomah Publishers, 2006).

Chapter 19: A Water Break

1. Isaiah 65:24 (NKJV).

2. Romans 1:20 (AMP).

3. Psalm 119:90 (NKJV).

4. Psalm 93:4a (KJV).

Chapter 20: A Woman Goes Fishing

1. Mark 1:17 (NKJV).

2. I Corinthians 9:22 (KJV).

3. Ephesians 2:4 (NKJV).

4. Psalm 100:5 (KJV).

5. John 6:51 (NKJV).

Chapter 21: Shearer Joy

1. Matthew 7:7 (KJV).

2. Proverbs 17:17, 18:24b (NKJV).

Chapter 22: School Daze

1. II Timothy 2:3 (KJV).

2. Isaiah 55:8 (KJV).

3. Lamentations 3:32 (NKJV).

4. Luke 9:57, 58 (NKJV).

5. Matthew 11:29.

6. Romans 5:3, 4 (NKJV).

7. Chambers, Oswald. *Approved Unto God*, combined volume (1946), delivered at the Bible Training College in London (delivered 1916). p. 113.

8. II Corinthians 1:3, 4 (NKJV).

Chapter 23: Celebrations

1. Revelation 3:18 (NKJV).

Chapter 24: I Will Build My Church

1. Ezekiel 3:17-19 (NKJV).

2. Proverbs 16:25 (NKJV).

3. I Thessalonians 5:24 (KJV).

Chapter 25: The Other Missionaries

1. I Corinthians 1:29 (NKJV).

Chapter 26: Last Two Letters Home

1. Psalm 91:11 (KJV).

Chapter 28: Reentry

1. I Samuel 2:30 (NKJV).

2. Hebrews 11:38 (NKJV).

Chapter 29: Back on the Couch

1. Jeremiah 13:23 (NKJV).

2. Psalm 138:8 (NKJV).

3. Spurgeon, C.H., *Cheque Book of the Bank of Faith* (Chicago: Moody Press, 1952), pg. 118.

Breinigsville, PA USA
12 April 2010
235950BV00002B/2/P